S0-AGM-119

GRAND CENTRAL
PUBLISHING

LARGE
PRINT

ALSO BY Christopher Buckley

Supreme Courtship

Boomsday

Florence of Arabia

No Way to Treat a First Lady

Washington Schlepped Here: Walking
in the Nation's Capital

Little Green Men

God Is My Broker

Wry Martinis

Thank You for Smoking

Wet Work

Campion

The White House Mess

Steaming to Bamboola: The World
of a Tramp Freighter

Losing Mum
and Pup

A MEMOIR

Christopher Buckley

TWELVE

LARGE PRINT

Copyright © 2009 by Christopher Taylor Buckley
All rights reserved. Except as permitted under the U.S. Copyright
Act of 1976, no part of this publication may be reproduced,
distributed, or transmitted in any form or by any means, or stored
in a database or retrieval system, without the prior written
permission of the publisher.

Twelve
Hachette Book Group
237 Park Avenue
New York, NY 10017

Visit our Web site at www.HachetteBookGroup.com.

Twelve is an imprint of Grand Central Publishing.
The Twelve name and logo are trademarks of Hachette Book
Group, Inc.

Printed in the United States of America

First Large Print Edition: May 2009
10 9 8 7 6 5 4 3 2 1

Library of Congress Cataloging-in-Publication Data

Buckley, Christopher
    Losing Mum and Pup : a memoir / Christopher Buckley.—1st ed.
    p. cm.
    ISBN 978-0-446-55239-4
    1. Buckley, Christopher, 1952—Family.   2. Authors, American—
20th century—Family relationships.   3. Parents—Death—
Psychological aspects.   4. Buckley, William F. (William Frank),
1925–2008—Last years.   5. Buckley, William F. (William Frank),
1925–2008—Death and burial.   I. Title.
    PS3552.U3394Z46 2009
    813'.54—dc22
    [B]   2008043532

The Large Print edition published in accord with the standards of
the N.A.V.H

for

Julian Booth

Frances Bronson

Danny Merritt

With love and gratitude

LADY BRACKNELL: . . . Are your parents living?

JACK: I have lost both my parents.

LADY BRACKNELL: Both? . . . To lose one parent, Mr. Worthing, may be regarded as a misfortune; to lose both looks like carelessness.

—Oscar Wilde,
The Importance of Being Earnest

I have put in italics conversations of whose accuracy I am reasonably confident, and within quotation marks those of whose accuracy I am entirely confident.

Losing Mum and Pup

You're Next

I'm not sure how this book will turn out. I mostly write novels, and I've found, having written half a dozen, that if you're lucky, the ending turns out a surprise and you wind up with something you hadn't anticipated in the outline. I suppose it's a process of outsmarting yourself (not especially hard in my case). Perhaps I'm outsmarting myself by writing this book at all. I'd pretty much resolved *not* to write a book about my famous parents. But I'm a writer, for better or worse, and when the universe hands you material like this, not writing about it seems either a waste or a conscious act of evasion.

By "material like this," I mean losing both your parents within a year. If that sounds callous or cavalier, it's not meant to be. My sins are manifold and blushful, but callousness and arrogance are not among them (at least, I hope not). The cliché is that a writer's life is his capital, and I find myself, as the funereal dust settles and the flowers dry, wanting—needing, perhaps more accurately—to try to make sense of it and put the year to rest, as I did my parents. Invariably, one seeks to move on. A book is labor, and as Pup taught me from a very early age—so early, indeed, that I didn't have the foggiest idea what he was talking about—"Industry is the enemy of melancholy." Now I get it.

There's this, too: My parents were not—with all respect to every other set of son-and-daughter-loving, wonderful parents in the wide, wide world—your average mom and dad. They were William F. Buckley Jr. and Patricia Taylor Buckley, both of them—and I hereby promise that this will be the only time I deploy this particular cliché—larger-than-life people. A gross understatement in their case. I wonder, having typed that: Is it name-dropping when they're your own parents?

But larger than life they both were, and then some. Larger than death, too, to judge from the public outpouring and from the tears of the people who loved them and mourn them and miss them, none more than their son, even if at times I was tempted to pack them off to earlier graves. Larger-than-life people create larger-than-life dramas.

To the extent this story has a larger-than-personal dimension, it is an account of becoming an orphan. I realize that "orphan" sounds like an overdramatic term for becoming parentless at age fifty-five; but I was struck by the number of times the word occurred in the eight hundred condolence letters I received after my father died. I hadn't thought of myself as an "orphan" until about the sixth or seventh letter: *Now you're an orphan. . . . I know the pain myself of being an orphan. . . . You must feel so lonely, being an orphan. . . . When I became an orphan it felt like the earth dropping out from under me.* At length a certain *froideur* encroached as the thought formed, *So, you're an orphan now.* I was jolted happily out of my thousand-yard stare a month later by an e-mail from my old pal Leon Wieseltier, to whom I'd written to say that I was finally headed off to Arizona for some R&R: "May your orphanhood be tanned."

Orphanhood was a condition I had associated with news stories of disasters; a theme I had examined intellectually in literature at college and beyond. It's one of the biggies, running through most of Melville, among others, and right down the middle of the great American novel *Adventures of Huckleberry Finn.*

I'm an only child, albeit encompassed and generously loved by an abundance of relatives, forty-nine first cousins on the Buckley side alone. Still, I have no sibling with whom to share my orphanhood, so perhaps the experience is more acutely felt. Only children often have more intense, or at least more tightly focused, relationships with their parents than children of larger families. This was, at any rate, my experience.

I don't know that I have anything

particularly useful, much less profound, to impart about the business of losing one's parents, other than this account of how it went in my case. I doubt you'll be stunned to hear that it has a somewhat dampening effect on one's general felicity and inclination to humor. I recall, on entering the vestibule of Leo P. Gallagher & Son Funeral Home the first time after Mum died, seeing a table stacked with pamphlets with titles like *Losing a Loved One* or *The Grieving Process,* illustrated with flowers and celestial sunbeams. As a satirist, which is to say someone who makes raspberries at the cosmos, my inclination is to parody: *Okay, They're Dead: Deal with It* or *Why It's Going to Cost You $7,000 to Cremate Mummy.* But standing there with my grief-stricken father, the banal suddenly didn't seem quite so silly or in need of a kick in the rear end, and (believe me) I'm a veteran chortler over Oscar Wilde's line "It would require a heart of stone not to laugh at the death of Little Nell." Right after JFK was shot, Mary McGrory said to Daniel Patrick Moynihan, "We'll never laugh again," to which Moynihan responded, "Mary, we'll laugh again, but we'll never be young again."

It occurs to me that Moynihan's reply brushes up against the nut of the orphanhood thing (as my former boss George H. W. Bush might put it)— namely, the accompanying realization that *you're next*. With the death of the second parent, one steps—or is not-so-gently nudged—across the threshold into the Green Room to the river Styx.

One of my early memories, age five, is of being in bed with my parents and being awoken in the middle of the night by the ringing of the phone. A great commotion of grown-ups followed: Mum going down to make coffee, Pup hunched over the phone, speaking in grave, urgent tones. Of course, I found it all exciting and eventful and hoped it would involve—with any luck—a reprieve from school that day. "What is it?" I asked Mum. "Pup's father has died, darling." Apart from being in the car when she drove over the family cocker spaniel, this was my first brush with death. Then, an even half century later, the phone rang again with the news that my father had died.

In the Zen koan, the noble lord sends word throughout the land, offering a huge reward to anyone who can distill for him in poetry the definition of happiness. (This was in the days before *Who Wants to Be a Millionaire?*) A monk duly shuffled in and handed the nobleman a poem that read, in its entirety:

> *Grandfather dies*
> *Father dies*
> *Son dies.*

His Lordship, having had in mind something a bit more, shall we say, upbeat, unsheathes his sword and is about to lop off the head of the impertinent divine. The monk says (in words to this effect), *Dude, chill! This is the definition of perfect happiness—that no father should outlive his son.* At this, His Lordship nods—or, more probably, after the fashion of Kurosawa's sixteenth-century warlords, grunts emphatically—and hands the monk a sack of gold. I'm sure the story reads more inspiringly in the original medieval Japanese, brush-painted on a silk scroll, but it's a nifty story, even as I now confront the fact that I have moved to the bottom line. My son, William Conor Buckley, whose namesake grandfather died on the morning of his sixteenth birthday, now himself moves one step closer to the Stygian Green Room, but if the old Zen monk's formula holds, he won't beat me to the river. Or so I, a heathen, fervently pray.

Many of those kind letters I received echoed another apparently universal aspect about parental mortality—namely, that no matter how much you prepare for the moment, when it comes, it comes at you hot, hard, and unrehearsed. Both my parents had been ill and suffering, so when the end came to each, it was technically a blessing. And yet there you stand in room 2 of the Stamford Hospital critical care unit, having just calmly given the order to remove the breathing tube, sobbing uncontrollably—sobbing, as distinct from crying or weeping—even though you spent eight hours in a car driving toward this scene, knowing pretty much what to expect. Then, ten months later, cradling the phone and wandering foggily and aimlessly about the house, wondering, almost like an actor trying to figure out how to play the scene: *Okay, you've just gotten word that your father is dead. You . . . let's see . . . punch the wall, shout, "Why? Why?"*—not quite knowing what to do, or say, or what gesture is called for. Something, surely? Before getting the call, I'd been on the way to my little study out back to do my income taxes. (Death and taxes, all in the same day. One reverts to childhood: *Go hide. Maybe they won't find you.* In the end, I just leaned my forehead against the inside of the front door, took in a few breaths, then walked upstairs to man the phones, which I knew would soon start to ring.

One thing I did learn that morning of February 27, 2008: In the Internet age, word travels fast. He died at 9:30. I called a friend at the *Times* and they had his (preprepared) obit up by 11:04. The president of the United States called me . . . it must have been before 11:30, anyway. Cyberspace doesn't give you a whole lot of time for collecting your thoughts. One well-meaning but a bit impetuous caller—it couldn't have been later than 11:15—demanded, repeatedly, to know what were the funeral arrangements, adding that he hoped it wouldn't complicate his trip to California. I was a tad brusque with the gentleman. My father was still lying warm on the floor of his study, awaiting the medical examiner, and I was being pressed for funeral plans. Perhaps one of the lessons of this book is: Don't feel too guilty for being a bit curt in these situations.

I do have one or two very concrete hopes for this book, which I'd like to get on the record, perhaps self-correctively, as I set out to write it. I *hope* to avoid any hint of self-pity, any sense that I've been dealt some unusually cruel hand. As I type this, 158 earthquake rescue workers in China have just been buried alive in a landslide; meanwhile, in benighted Myanmar, hundreds of thousands are perishing horribly at the hands of ghastly tyrants; my best friend's son—my own godson—is in harm's way with the U.S. Army in Iraq; his brother is soon en route there. I have—*touch wood!* as Mum used to say—health and wealth. I say a secular grace before meals and count my myriad blessings. *My cup runneth over*, as Pup used to say. I can't say this past year has been a laugh riot. I've quoted Queen Elizabeth's *annus horribilis* line once or twice. But if at any point you hear a whimpering of *oh, poor little me*, just chuck the book right into the wastebasket—or better yet, take it back and exchange it for a fresh paperback copy of *Running with Scissors*.

My other hope is that the book will be, despite its not exactly upbeat subject matter, a celebration—as we insist, in our smiley-faced times, on denominating funeral and memorial services—of two extraordinary people, my Mum and Pup; and that it will be worthy of them, even if some parts of it would no doubt appall them. For public people, they could be rather private. But then one advantage to orphanhood, however bittersweet, is that for better or worse it's your call now.

CHAPTER 1

April Is the Cruelest Month

❧

April 14, 2007, began well enough. I was at Washington and Lee University in very rural Lexington, Virginia. It has a beautiful campus, and the occasion was an egotist's wet dream. The previous afternoon, I had driven into town underneath a enormous banner slung across the main street: CHRISTOPHER

BUCKLEY'S WASHINGTON—THE TOM WOLFE LECTURE SERIES. Hot diggity dog. A two-day program of talks and seminars by professors of journalism and political science, all about my novels, ending with a lecture by Tom Wolfe, on the topic of same. It doesn't get any better than that. Tom Wolfe has been my beau ideal and hero since 1970, when at age seventeen I came upon his *Electric Kool-Aid Acid Test* and stayed up all night, silent upon a peak in Darien, inhaling his nitrous-injected prose. So, sweeping all modesty aside, I found being invited to this event at W and L— the Maestro's own alma mater—very cool indeed.

The night before, after my talk, there had been a reception at the president's house. I asked my host if this had in fact been Robert E. Lee's house when he was president of Washington College, as it was then called. The answer was yes, and furthermore, it was in this very room, the dining room, that he had died. He was stricken at mealtime and, unable to be moved, had spent his final days there.

I looked about the room reverently. Death was on my mind. It was April 13, just four days after the anniversary of the surrender at Appomattox, not so far from here; it was, as well, the eve of the anniversary of the assassination of Abraham Lincoln, Lee's old foe.* On the walk to dinner after the reception, I was shown the stable where Lee's horse, Traveller, had spent his last days. I'd asked to see it because I had once owned a small wooden sailboat that I'd named *Traveller*, after him. My Buckley grandmother, a proud native of New Orleans (born 1895), stoutly maintained that we are related to Robert E. Lee,

---

*I recall thinking, at the time, that April 14 was also the day the *Titanic* hit the iceberg. Clearly, some negative energy hangs over the date.

but my uncle Reid, the family historian, has laid that pretty fiction firmly to rest. The Buckleys are related to Robert E. Lee in roughly the same sense that every human being on the planet is related to that procreative hominid lady who lived in Africa a hundred thousand years ago. Reid did, on the other hand, establish that Mimi's grandfather was decorated for bravery fighting for Lee at Shiloh, as well as on subsequent other killing fields. Relatives of Robert E. Lee are as numerous as crew members of JFK's torpedo boat PT-109.[*]

There was a screening after the dinner of *Thank You for Smoking*, a movie adapted from one of the aforementioned Washington novels. Having seen it more times than there are relatives of Robert E. Lee, I ducked out early and

---

[*]Someone once calculated that enough people claimed to have served aboard Lieutenant (JG) Kennedy's boat to man an aircraft carrier.

walked back to the little guesthouse up the hill. My cell phone showed no bars, and I was anxious to see if there were any messages. My mother was dying 450 miles north of here, and I felt isolated, all the more so for the deep, cicada-loud country night.

This was Friday. (The 13th, it occurs.) On Tuesday, she had gone into the hospital to have a stent installed in her thigh in hopes of preventing further amputations. Thursday, the wound went septic. She lapsed into a coma from which the doctors said she would not emerge. Over the phone on Friday morning, Pup had said to me, *Go to Virginia. Honor the commitment. There's no point in coming up.* Then he'd said, *Why don't we agree that the next call you get from me will be when she's dead.*

I didn't know what to say to that. Pup's fatalism could sometimes border on sangfroid. He had over the course of his life given (literally) thousands of speeches, and he had a paladin code of conduct that the show must go on. My inclination was to speed to the side of my mother, whether she was sensate or not. But the Wolfe event had been laid on months ago; hundreds of people had been paid money and come long distances. Still, I demurred, if only for practical reasons: I imagined myself mounting the podium to make the audience laugh (my one talent) moments after getting a phone call informing me that my mother had just died. But Pup was adamant. *She's in a coma, Big Shot. She wouldn't know you're there. Go.* So I put down the phone and cried and went to Virginia.

Now, Saturday morning, I sat in the audience and listened to Tom Wolfe say nice things about my work. I'd known him for about thirty years. I blush to admit that I had importuned him for blurbs for my early books, which he had quite correctly declined to provide.

(Oh, Youth: What an utter *ass* you can be!) Many years later, Tom indicated, more than generously, his approval, which was all the sweeter for its having been long in the coming.

There was a lunch, but I had to skip that because a car was waiting to get me to Baltimore, five hours away, for the next gig, the annual fund-raiser at the Enoch Pratt Free Library. I was the speaker. That too had been arranged months in advance and had been heavily promoted. I said grateful good-byes to my hosts and to the Man in White, drove out under the CHRISTOPHER BUCKLEY'S WASHINGTON banner, and, seeing bars on my cell phone, phoned my wife, Lucy, in Washington.

She told me the death watch had begun. Pup had announced he would not return to the hospital. Uncle Jimmy and Aunt Pitts had come down from Sharon to be with him, but they had now gone back. Jimmy's wife, Ann, had been paralyzed from the neck down in an awful car accident, and he didn't like to leave her for long. Pitts, who is to the Buckley family what Gibraltar is to the Mediterranean, had told Lucy, *I think Christo better get back.* So I hung up with Lucy and called the lady at the Enoch Pratt Free Library.

"Oh, yes, Mr. Buckley," she said merrily, "we're so looking forward to seeing you."

I blurted, "My mother isn't expected to live out the night." I choked up halfway through. I can't account for where such stilted language came from. They're words that you might hear in a hospital soap opera. I don't talk like that. It leaves me wondering if, in such situations, one subconsciously plagiarizes from remembered dialogue left in the brain's attic.

There was a pause. She said, "Of course. I'm so sorry."

I felt awful screwing things up so for

the library. But as cancellation excuses go, a dying mother is pretty unassailable. It *should* be, at any rate. But then I remember a story told me by a friend, the sister of a hugely successful movie producer: Her brother was summoned, along with other family members, to the bed of their dying mother. He was at the time shooting a big-budget movie that you have almost certainly seen. No sooner had he arrived in the hospital room in New York than the two studio heads phoned him—"screaming, I mean, *screaming*," she said—at him to fly back to the set. You'd recognize their names. Still wanna be in showbiz?

There was a storm moving in from the west, rain coming down harder and harder. *Right,* I thought, *the objective correlative: the outward aspect mirroring the inner aspect.* (Once an English major, always an English major.) I phoned Lucy back. The airports were shutting down. There was no point in trying to fly. I could make Washington in four hours and catch an Acela train to Stamford, but that wouldn't get me in until late. At this point the driver, whose card gave his name as Shuja Qureshi, overhearing my fraught negotiations, piped up in an Indian accent: "Sir? *I* can drive you to Stamford, Conneck-ti-cut." Okay, I said. Let's go. He stabbed the buttons on his dash-mounted GPS and reported that it would take eight hours. I sat back, mind reeling. *Industry is the enemy of melancholy.* So I opened my laptop and composed an obituary that could be sent out to the newspapers to help them with the details.

PATRICIA TAYLOR BUCKLEY

At the Stamford (Conn.) Hospital, of a [[TK]], following a long illness. [[TK time]]

---

*TK is journalist shorthand for information "to come."

Born Vancouver, British Columbia, Canada, July 1, 1926. Father: Austin Cotterell Taylor. Mother: Kathleen Elliott Taylor. Her father was a self-made industrialist whose racehorses Indian Broom and Wychcee competed against Seabiscuit. Mr. Taylor died in 1965.* Her mother, a civic leader in Vancouver, died in 1972. Mrs. Buckley's maternal grandfather was chief of police of Winnipeg, Manitoba. Mrs. Buckley's brother, financier Austin G. E. Taylor of Vancouver, died in 1996. Her sister Kathleen Finucane, of Vancouver, died in March.

Patricia Aldyen Austin Taylor was educated at Crofton House School, Vancouver. She attended Vassar College, where she met

---

*On Election Day, when my father ran for mayor of New York.

her future husband through her roommate Patricia Buckley. She and her roommate's older brother, William F. Buckley Jr., were married in Vancouver on July 6, 1950, in what was then the largest wedding in the city's history.

Mrs. Buckley went from the life of a debutante to a vacuum cleaner-wielding wife of a junior faculty member of Yale. She and Mr. Buckley lived in Hamden, Connecticut, while he wrote his first book, God and Man at Yale, *while working as a junior instructor in the Spanish Department. After Mr. Buckley served a brief stint in Mexico City with the Central Intelligence Agency—his superior was E. Howard Hunt, later of Watergate break-in fame—he and his wife settled in Stamford, Connecticut, their home ever since. Their only child, Christo-*

pher Taylor Buckley, was born in 1952.

Mrs. Buckley became a leading member of New York society and was active in numerous charities and civic causes. She raised money for various hospitals, including St. Vincent's. She served on many boards and was an honorary director of the Metropolitan Museum of Art. For many years, she chaired the annual dinner of the Museum's Costume Institute.

Pat Buckley moved easily amidst notables from the worlds of politics, literature, the arts, philanthropy, fashion, and society. Her friends included Henry and Nancy Kissinger, Ronald and Nancy Reagan, Jerome Zipkin, Betsy Bloomingdale, Nan Kempner, Clare Boothe Luce, Bill Blass, Tammany leader Carmine DeSapio, Abe Rosenthal and Shir-

ley Lord, Mrs. Gary "Rocky" Cooper, David Niven, John Kenneth Galbraith, Sir Harry Evans and Tina Brown, (British director) Peter Glenville, Princess Grace of Monaco, Don Juan de Borbon (father of the present King of Spain), publisher John Fairchild, Richard Avedon, Dominick Dunne, Bob Colacello, Sir Alistair Horne, Aileen Mehle, Richard and Shirley Clurman, John and Drue Heinz, Reinaldo and Carolina Herrera, Tom Wolfe, Taki and Alexandra Theadoracopulos, Clay Felker, Ahmet and Mica Ertegun, C.Z. Guest, Kenneth J. Lane, Valentino, Halston, Walter Cronkite, Mike Wallace, David Halberstam, Vladimir Nabokov, Roger Moore, Truman Capote, Rosalyn Tureck, Alicia de Larrocha, James Clavell, King Constantine of Greece, Malcolm Forbes Sr., Brooke Astor,

Anne Slater, Mortimer's owner Glen Birnbaum, among others.

Rereading this now, I'm amused by that "among others." Who could I possibly have left out of this bold-face cornucopia?

She was known for her exacting taste in everything from clothes to decorating and food. She maintained a notably slender figure—Women's Wear Daily often referred to her as the "chic and stunning Mrs. Buckley"—and to her "belle poitrine." She was an early booster of—and walking advertisement for—American designers, particularly Bill Blass. A regular on the Best Dressed List, she was inducted into its Hall of Fame in the 1990s. She favored costume jewelry made by her gin rummy pal Kenneth J. Lane. In his memoir, Mr. Blass noted that he and Mrs. Buckley would occasionally play hooky from their hectic schedules in order to see as many movies as they could back-to-back in one day, "an operation that required near-military planning."

Despite her elegant figure, Mrs. Buckley was a famous foodie (a term she herself would never have used). Unable to boil a three-minute egg at the time she married, she dutifully took cooking classes with James Beard. In the 1970s, she became a champion of Glorious Food, the now famous catering firm started by Sean Driscoll. She refined her skills as a giver of fancy benefit dinners for up to 1,000 people by improvising "Pat's Pot Pie," a chicken pot pie that eliminated the time-consuming need for serving veg-

etables and sauces separately. It was an innovation hailed by her famously impatient husband.

Over the years, Mrs. Buckley acted as a kind of den mother to the conservative movement, giving dinners to the editors of her husband's magazine, National Review, *every other Monday, starting in the mid-1960s. At her husband's 80th birthday celebration in 2005 at the Pierre Hotel in New York, her son, Christopher, noted in a toast that "No one ever left my mother's house less than well and truly stuffed."*

Though she was often in the limelight, Mrs. Buckley tended to shy from it, content to leave center stage to her husband. She often said, "I'm just a simple country girl from the woods of British Columbia," though by any account she was anything but simple and had long since left the woods of her native British Columbia.

She is survived by her husband of 57 years, William F. Buckley Jr. of Stamford, CT; her son, Christopher Taylor Buckley, of Washington, D.C.; granddaughter, Caitlin Gregg Buckley, and grandson, William Conor Buckley.

Shuja and I stopped at a McDonald's. We sat across from each other, eating our Big Macs and fries. *Grease is the enemy of melancholy.* I would put on quite a few extra pounds in the days ahead, justifying it as perfectly okay under the circumstances. *Your mother died. Go ahead, eat all you want.*

"What is the matter with your mother?" Shuja said between bites.

"She's dying," I said.

It just came out. It was the second time I couldn't account for my words. He nodded and gave a sympathetic tilt of the head and took another bite of his Big Mac. I felt embarrassed for him.

"I really like McDonald's," I said, trying to change the subject.

"Oh, yes . . ." Shuja brightened. "McDonald's is *excellent*."

CHAPTER 2

She's Already in Heaven

We pulled into Stamford eight hours later, just after nine o'clock. Danny, my best friend since age thirteen, was waiting for me. He became, over the years, a sort of second son to my father. He reported that Pup had gone to bed. He was not in good health (emphysema, diabetes, sleep apnea) and normally went upstairs after dinner by about eight-fifteen, aboard his new stairway rail chair. He would then, typically, take the first of numerous sleeping pills. (Pup's self-medication would be a big theme in the coming year.) Tonight, before he went upstairs, he had said to Danny, several times, *Why is Christo going to the hospital? She's in a coma. She won't know he's there.* Danny—kindly, patient, good Danny—said to him, *Bill, he wants to say good-bye to his mother.*

He drove me to Stamford Hospital. He told me that although Pup had declared that he wouldn't go there, he had, twice, each time driving himself. I winced at hearing this, since I'd given covert but imperative instructions to Danny and the staff that they must not, under any circumstances, let Pup get behind the wheel of a car. A moving vehicle was now, in his hands, a potential weapon of mass destruction far more minatory than anything in the arsenal of Saddam Hussein or Kim Jong-il. But gone to the hospital he had, and for that I was glad; glad, too, not to have been there when he said good-bye to her. His grief would only have been a distraction. This is perhaps cruel, but it's true: acute grief is best one-on-one.

Danny left me at the door to the critical care unit. The nurse buzzed me in. I entered her room. The chic and stunning Mrs. Buckley lay on her bed, shrunken, eyes open and unseeing, a thick plastic respirator tube protruding from her mouth, making a loud, rhythmic, bellows-noise as it injected and drew air from her lungs. I lost it and began to sob. The nurse kindly left.

I drew up a chair and held what I could of her hand, which was cold and bony and edematous with fluid. The nurse returned shortly and said that Dr. D'Amico was on the phone. Joe D'Amico was her orthopedist, a kindly, attentive, and warm man. The week before, he had amputated three mummified toes on her left foot. She'd stubbed them the previous November and, having fallen and broken so many bones in her body over the years, she had, in the fashion of Victorian ladies, simply taken to her bed to die. Six months of lying there, on top of sixty-five years of smoking, does not a robust cardio-aerobic regime make. The toes, deprived of circulation, had gone dry-gangrenous. Odd, I reflect now: She had always maintained an exquisite figure—a truly striking figure—and yet I can't remember a single instance of her ever breaking a sweat.

Joe came on the line. He said how sorry he was, that she was a wonderful lady. He said, *What you're seeing there isn't her. She's already in heaven.*

Joe and I had never discussed religion. I doubt, for that matter, that he and she had ever discussed it. Mum was nominally Anglican, dutifully attending church on Easter and Christmas. She would, even more dutifully, have the local pastor, a sweet old bore, over for lunch once or twice a year. On these occasions, she would instruct her New York houseguests—uniformly consisting of witty, fun, elegant, and gay gentlemen: "Now don't leave me alone with him!"

I don't think I ever once heard Mum utter a religious or spiritual sentiment, a considerable feat considering that she was married for fifty-seven years to one of the most prominent Catholics in the country. But she observed the proprieties with old-world de rigueur. When Pup taped a *Firing Line* in the Sistine Chapel with Princess Grace, Malcolm Muggeridge, Charlton Heston, and David Niven, Mum was included in the post-taping audience with Pope John Paul II. There's a photo of the occasion: She has on more black lace than a Goya duchess; the effect is that of the Magdalene, as dressed by Bill Blass.

I don't to this day know if Dr. Joe D'Amico is religious, but I didn't mind his phraseology. *She's already in heaven* is a gentle way of saying, *She's gone and she's not coming back.* (My parents loved the joke about the tactless army sergeant instructed to break the news gently to Private Jones: *All right, men, I want everyone with a living mother to take one step forward— NOT SO FAST, JONES!*) Death is an occasion of hushed tones and nursery talk. In the scene in Evelyn Waugh's *Brideshead Revisited* in which Lord Marchmain lies dying, his Italian mistress, Cara, trying to get him to accept last rites, strokes his forehead and speaks to him softly: "Alex, you remember the priest from Melstead. You were very naughty with him when he came to see you. You hurt his feelings very much. Now he's here again. . . ."

I stammered out my thanks to Joe for everything he'd done for her. He asked, *Do you want to leave the respirator in or let nature take its course?* I said, *Let's remove the respirator.*

I'd brought with me a pocket copy of the Book of Ecclesiastes. The line in *Moby-Dick* had lodged long ago in my mind: "The truest of all men was the Man of Sorrows, and the truest of all books is Solomon's, and Ecclesiastes is the fine hammered steel of woe." I'd grabbed it off my bookshelf on the way to Virginia, figuring that a little fine-hammered steel would probably be a good thing to have on this trip. I'm agnostic now, but I haven't quite reached the point of reading aloud from Richard Dawkins's *The God Delusion* at the deathbed of a loved one.

I was reading the ancient text aloud to my unhearing mother when after a few moments I became aware that someone had entered the room and was standing by the foot of the bed. He introduced himself to me as Dr. So-and-So and, shaking his head with what seemed genuine perplexity, said, *I just don't understand how this could have happened*. He then launched into an interminable—five, six minutes, seven minutes?—and detailed account of how the stent operation had gone wrong. I wasn't taking notes at the time and so can't recapitulate it, but it was highly technical. He went on and on—using abstruse medical terms, as if he were explaining it all to a colleague. All I could do was nod and repeat, *Thank you . . . thank you . . . I really appreciate all you did for her . . .* But he wouldn't leave, would not be deterred from explaining every minute vascular aspect of the surgery, until, toward minute eight or nine it dawned on me: *He's apologizing for killing her.* I muttered, *It's all right,* and it was: This wasn't a young woman with her whole life in front of her. Whatever had gone wrong in the OR, it was a blessing. Putting in the stent was an attempt to stave off further amputation. The thought of my elegant, beautiful Mum enduring some death of a hundred cuts was too much to contemplate. She'd once said to me, only half-kidding, "I've got the best legs in the business." And she did—she *did*. But now I just wanted this doctor to go away and leave us alone.

Finally, having exhausted himself lexicographically, he began to make his exit. I thanked him one last time. As I write this, the *Times* is reporting on the front page that more and more doctors are apologizing for their mistakes, and—what do you know—it's cut down on the filing of malpractice suits. Perhaps, after all, the most beautiful words in the language are *I'm sorry*.

We were alone again, briefly, until another doctor arrived to remove the respirator. He said, "You might not want to be here for this." No, I didn't. I went out into the corridor and hovered. I should have walked to the end of it. The sound as a respirator is removed isn't one you want to hear. But it was quiet and peaceful in the room when I returned, just the pings and beeps emanating from the monitor. I stroked her hair and said, the words surprising me, coming out of nowhere, "I forgive you."

It sounded—even to me, at the time—like a terribly presumptuous statement, but it needed to be said. She never would have asked for forgiveness herself, even in extremis. She was far too proud. Only once or twice, when she had been truly awful, had she apologized to me. Generally, she was defiant—almost magnificently so—when her demons slipped their leash. Lucy, wise Lucy, had the rule *Don't go to bed angry*. Now, watching Mum go to bed for the last time, I didn't want any anger left between us, so out came the unrehearsed words. For my sake more than for hers. Well, if she was already in heaven, it was all moot anyway. Right?

The doctor had said after removing the tube, "It usually goes quickly." I sat beside her, watching the monitor, with its numbers and differently colored lines and chirps that tracked her breathing and heartbeat and other diminishing vitals. Her heart rate would slow, then quicken, then slow. After some minutes, I realized that I had become fixated on the monitor. I heard her saying to me—a half century earlier: *Are you just going to sit there and watch* television *all day?* It would have been some spectacularly sunny Saturday morning, and I was glued to the telly (her term for it), watching Johnny Weissmuller nodding in agreement as the remarkably intelligible chimp Cheeta explained to him that Jane was being held hostage by evil Belgian ivory hunters 3.4 miles north-northwest of the abandoned mine. I read, sometime after, that monitor fixation is routine in death watches: We have become, even in death, TV watchers.

Her heart rate and respiration slowed. It didn't requicken. I texted on my cell phone to Lucy: "End near."

Just before two o'clock in the morning on April 15, the respiratory line indicated that her breathing had stopped. Yet her heart continued to beat, according to the faint but distinct blips. I rushed to find the nurse. *It's normal,* she said. *It takes a little while.* She examined the monitor, held Mum's wrist, and nodded. It was over.

She went to fetch the doctor so he could "pronounce." He arrived, held a pen flashlight to her eyes, put a stethoscope to her chest. *I'm sorry,* he said. Did I want an autopsy? No. My journalistic training kicked in as I remembered the "TK" in my obituary. What had she died of? I volunteered, "Natural causes?"

thinking to provide cover for the apologetic doctor and Stamford Hospital, for whom I had nothing but gratitude and praise. "No," he said, "infection. She died of infection." I winced at the thought of entering, "at two a.m., of infection. . . ." Surely one of the least attractive (Mum's term) words in the language. Couldn't we get away with "after a long illness"? It had certainly been that, too.

I noticed the doctor's name on his ID badge. It sounded exotic. I asked where he was from. "Macedonia," he said almost warily, as if that required some explaining. I managed not to say, "Alexander the Great."

He left us alone. I stroked her forehead for a while, as she used to mine, and spoke a few words to her, which, strangely, I cannot remember. Words of good-bye, I suppose they were. I tried to close her eyes. In the movies, they close. In real life, they don't. This is why in the old days they would put coins over the lids. I pulled the sheet up over her face, which had the effect of transforming the room from a state-of-the-art medical site into a funeral parlor. I took my last look at her and left.

Danny found me sitting by the emergency front door, weeping onto my opened laptop as I e-mailed out the obituary to the first wave of recipients. We drove home through empty Stamford streets. We tried to wake Pup, but by now he had taken enough sleeping pills to narcotize a rhino, so I left a note by his bed that said, "Mum's suffering is over," drank two stiff Bloody Marys with Danny, and went to bed in the room I grew up in, listening to the rain against the windows and watching the branches of the tall pine tree I used to climb sway wildly in the wind.

CHAPTER 3

I Guess We Can Do Anything We Want To

Pup woke me about eight-thirty, calling from his garage study. I'd e-mailed him the obituary before going to sleep. He said how glad he was to have it. He'd always been encouraging and complimentary about my writing—and just as often critical. Pup was generous, if a tough grader. But in recent years, he had found it increasingly difficult, if not impossible, to compliment something I'd written, unless it was about him. (I say this with bemusement now, but at the time it wasn't all that bemusing.) Of my last book, a novel published two weeks before Mum died and which reviewers were (for the most part) describing as my best to date, he'd confined his comments in an e-mail P.S.: "This one didn't work for me. Sorry."

I walked to his study and tried to give him a hug, though it was hard to reach him through all the clutter and Jaime. Pup had occupied this converted garage space since 1952, and except for the papers serially shipped up to Yale over the years, he hadn't thrown away anything, with the result that the study had become a *son et lumière* exhibit that might be titled "The William F. Buckley Jr. Experience." (About a year later, I would find myself cleaning out this truly Augean stable. One week and two Dumpsters later, I had only scratched the surface.)

Jaime was Pup's computer factotum. They spoke Spanish exclusively. He seemed always to be there, possibly owing to Pup's Rube Goldberg computer habits. In 2008, he was probably the only human left on the planet who still used WordStar, the word-processing system he had learned in 1983. Loading WordStar into his up-to-date Dell computer was akin to installing the controls of a Sopwith Camel in a F-16 fighter jet, but Pup could not be budged from his WordStar. Generations of WFB amanuenses had to learn this cuneiform in order to edit his manuscripts and articles.

He was, on this dreary, rain-swept Sunday morning, red-eyed, puffy-faced, out of breath, in rough shape. He was gradually suffocating from emphysema and had just lost his wife of fifty-seven years. We embraced as best we could amid the office and Jaime jam. I glanced at his computer screen. He'd been stabbing at the keyboard, composing an e-mail alert about Mum's death. There were multiple typos. Her name was misspelled. In recent years, Pup's e-mails had become celebrated among his many correspondents for their increasing inscrutability. Once one of the most expert and accurate touch typists in the land, he now simply put his hands over the keyboard wherever they fell and commenced typing—and kept *on* typing—with the result that his e-mails often read like coded transmissions from a submarine:

Daer cgurisito,
Am sO hpinyg yiy wiutgh jw her for thep conserg tyjis friady!!! xxP
   [Trans.: Dear Christo, I am so very happy you will be at the concert on Friday.]

I teased him that he ought to provide his correspondents with Enigma machines in order to decode these transmissions. Once, despairing of being able to decipher a single word, I wrote back, "Dear Pup, I honestly am eager to know what you say here, but I just can't make it out." He called back and said, laughing, "I can't tell what it's about, either." I cleaned up the spelling of Mum's name on his e-mail. Age six, I had sat on his lap right here in this room and learned to touch-type, "The quick brown fox jumped over the lazy cow," on his old Royal typewriter.

The storm was still blowing. Pup, Danny, and I went out to lunch at Jimmy's Seaside Tavern. We ordered Bloody Marys and beers and wine and Reuben sandwiches and onion rings. "Shall we go see a flick?" he said, and the words brought me back a half century. Summer evenings after dinner when I was

little, he'd say, "Shall we go see a flick?"
I'd race to get the *Stamford Advocate*
with the movie listings. We'd jump into
the car and make it to the theater just
as the movie was starting. Within five
minutes he'd be snoring like a chain
saw. Mum would poke him—"Ducky,
wake up"—whereupon Ducky would
snort back to consciousness, look up
at Gary Cooper (or whoever) on the
screen, and demand in a loud voice,
"Ducky, who *is* that man? What is he
doing?"

I said to him, "Well, sure, why not?"

He smiled in a funny way and said, "I
guess we can do anything we *want* to."
It occurred to me, looking at him, that
it was the first time in fifty-seven years
he didn't have to wonder what Mum
might say. He could—yes—do whatever
he wanted; not that he hadn't always—I
chuckle a bit darkly as I type—but that
droit du seigneur autonomy had come
at considerable cost. We didn't go to a

movie after all. He was tired and needed a nap. About five o'clock, Danny rang me from his apartment over the garage study to say that Pup was going to mass. I said I'd come.

Normally, I didn't. Normally, when home of a Sunday, I would discreetly make myself scarce around this time, when he would gather up the Hispanic staff and drive to St. Mary's Church, where a complaisant priest would say a private Latin mass for him. Pup was a defiantly pre-Vatican II Catholic. One of the reforms of Vatican II, along with a perfectly comprehensible but perfectly bland liturgy, is the Sign of Peace, at which the priest urges the congregants to turn to one another and shake hands, or kiss, hug, high-five, power dap, whatever. Pup, despite his paradigmatically generous Christian-ity, found this "kumbaya" beyond the pale, and ten seconds in advance, he would preemptively drop to his knees

and bury his face in his hands in per-
fervid orison.

Today, however, I reckoned, was not
a day to skip church, so I went with
them in the still-sheeting rain. Pup
wept throughout the mass. Afterward
he told Danny, our go-between, that he
was "so pleased" I had attended.

Pup and I had engaged in our own
Hundred Years' War over the matter
of faith. Finally exhausted, I had—
whether hypocritically or cowardly or
wisely—put on a *Potemkin* facade of
being back in the fold. My agnosticism,
once defiant, had gone underground. I
no longer had the desire to nail my the-
ses to his church door. By now I knew
we didn't have much time left, and I
didn't want to spend it locking theological antlers, making him heartsick with
my intransigence.

It's only now, after his death, that I'm
able to write about this, without fear
of initiating another cannonade volley

of (all-*too*-intelligible) e-mails on the subject of my eternal damnation.[*] Our sturmiest und drangiest times were over religion. Pup had the most delicious, reliable, wicked, vibrant sense of humor of anyone I knew, yet his inner Savonarola was released at the merest hint of (to use his term) impiety. I was never, even in the fullest bloom of my agnosticism, a mocker—more the bemused skeptic. I've written both a serious play[†] about a sixteenth-century Catholic martyr and a comic novel[††] about some corrupt winemaking monks. The latter was an affectionate farce. I

---

[*]H. L. Mencken, to whose writings Pup introduced me, was proudly atheist but wrote that "If I am wrong, I will square myself when confronted in afterlife by the apostles with the simple apology, 'Gentlemen, I was wrong.'"

[†]*Campion,* performed at the Williamstown Theatre Festival, 1987.

[††]*God Is My Broker,* coauthored with my college pal John Tierney.

myself spent four years at a monastic New England boarding school and look back on it with great fondness and abundant admiration for many of the monks who suffered through those four years of me.

As for the novel, Pup did not find the humor in it, though others were chuckling. An uncle of mine, every inch as pious as Pup, said to me at his son's wedding, "That is the funniest darn book I have ever read!" I pointed to Pup, across the room, and said, "Do me a favor, would you? Tell him what you just told me." Uncle Gerry scurried off enthusiastically on his evangelical assignment, only to return, shrugging. "What did he say?" "He just stared at me."

I remember Pup's telling me, in 1981 as we trudged up the snowy lawn after scattering the ashes of his beloved friend and column syndicator, Harry Elmlark, *"Ojalá que hubiera sido Católico."* (If only he had been a Catholic.) Pup and I often spoke in Spanish—his first language—when we had intimacies to convey. Harry was a Jew and about the furthest thing from a Catholic as one could be, though come to think of it, he had been happily married to one all his life. I recall being stunned by the statement. I said, "What do you mean, Pup?" He replied matter-of-factly that as Harry was not Catholic, he had no expectation of seeing him again in heaven. This truly hit me like a smack in the face. Pup loved Harry wholeheartedly, but rules were—apparently—rules: The gates of heaven were shut against nonbelievers. I was crushed, for I too had loved Harry. I was, at the time (age twenty-eight), very much a believer, and I tended to take Pup's theological pronouncements as having ex cathedra papal authority.

Sometime later, he spoke—with genuine relief in his voice—of his discovery of a loophole called "the doctrine of invincible ignorance," which, if I understand it—theological half-gainers can leave a lad's head spinning at times—means that the normal rules with respect to admission to heaven are suspended *if* you are incapable intellectually or culturally of accepting that the Catholic Church is the one true Church, the only means of redemption. How Pup smiled with relief as he explained it across the lunch table that summer day!

Catholic theology is generally thought to be rigid—and indeed is on certain points—but sometimes Mother Church thinks like a $700-an-hour lawyer. One doesn't hear the word *Jesuitical* as much as one used to, but I found myself, during the Clinton years, musing on the fact that the president who gave us "It depends on what the meaning of the word *is* is" was educated at the nation's leading Jesuit university. I suppose it's worth mentioning that the celebrated English-speaking saint

Thomas More was himself a very clever lawyer.

Pup's faith was in a sense binary. He had imbibed his catechism at the knee of a deeply devout New Orleans Catholic lady who instilled in him what Chesterton and Waugh called the nursery-story aspect of Christianity. His father was a stern, perhaps even forbidding, but deep-down loving and affectionate Texan, the son of a hardscrabble-poor, sheep-farming sheriff. But exigent and unbending though Pup's faith was, he was himself the son of a lawyer and could find his own loopholes if it came to that. Perhaps his own heart was the largest of the loopholes. In 1996, speaking at the Fifth Avenue Synagogue memorial service for his great friend Dick Clurman, he ended his eulogy with a line I can quote today from memory: "It occurs to me that all my life I have unconsciously been on the lookout for the perfect Christian, and when I found him, he turned out to be a non-observant Jew."

"YES, MR. BUCKLEY, I have you and Dad down for eleven o'clock." At the funeral home, that is.

You and Dad. Pup and I had a giggle over that.

We stopped en route at Dunkin' Donuts. As we pulled into the parking lot, Pup's cell phone trilled. He fumbled it open, listened, and said, "Get a time and I'll call back." Inside, waiting for our iced coffees, he looked up at the TV screen, which showed President Bush. Pup said, "He just called. *Very* thoughtful."

I agreed that it was, extremely so. Later, when we returned to the house from the funeral home, it turned out that it had been President Bush 41, calling not for him, but for me. (I had worked for George Herbert Walker

Bush when he was vice president.) As a fan of Stephen Potter, author of the *Upmanship* books, I could hardly let this go to waste. I waited for the right moment at lunch and said, "Oh, by the way, that was my President Bush, calling for me." Okay, maybe you had to be there, but it was the day after my mother died and you take your laughs where you can find them. Pup, who himself held a tenth-degree black belt in Upmanship, wasn't quite sure whether to be amused by my remark. He had been on the receiving end of many, many calls from presidents of the United States; not to mention that *my* Bush had awarded him the Medal of Freedom in 1991. (Touché, I can hear Pup saying.) One morning, during the Nixon administration, the phone rang in Stamford at what Mum deemed an inappropriately early hour on a Sunday. "The president is calling for Mr. Buckley," the voice announced. Mum fired back in her most formidable voice—and trust me when I say formidable: a cross between Noel Coward and a snapping turtle—"The president of *what?*" To which the White House operator calmly replied, "Our *country*, ma'am."

I didn't return the call from *my* Bush but instead sent an e-mail to his assistant Linda, saying that I was touched but not yet ready to talk, being unconfident of my emotions. I knew he'd understand. I had called him at Camp David in December 1992, after his own mother had died. I was writing a piece about her for *The New Yorker.* Between his mother's death, his impending departure from the White House, and running the country, Mr. Bush had a lot on his plate, but being the generous soul he is, he took the call. In the course of reminiscing about Dorothy Bush, the petite but also formidable Bush family matriarch, the president alluded to his membership in something called "the Bawl Brigade." I inferred this consisted of Bushes who cry easily. George Herbert Walker Bush is, surely, the honorary colonel of this moist brigade. I learned early on while writing speeches for him (between 1981 and 1983) that he may be a New England Yankee blue blood, but he has the tear ducts of a Sicilian grandmother. The man mists up during the playing of "The Star-Spangled Banner" on opening day at the ball park. I can't imagine what tears flowed when, as a young navy wartime aviator, he watched comrades killed or, as a young father, endured the death of his six-year-old daughter from leukemia.

"No me digas nada triste," Pup said as we sat around the conference table at Leo P. Gallagher & Son Funeral Home. (Don't say anything sad to me.) He was afraid of breaking down in front of the young funeral director—named, as it happened, Chris. Chris was gentle-mannered,

considerate, and punctilious. But then I suppose rudeness and brusqueness are not considered prize qualities in the funeral-directing business. In the presence of death, one craves the soft touch, the lowered voice, even if it verges on the baroque. I remember reading in the memoirs of one of my favorite actors, Richard E. Grant (*Withnail and I*), the gruesome moment when a hospital worker holding a box containing his newborn son's corpse shoved it at him with all the tenderness of a grouchy janitor handling a bag of garbage. (A vignette like that sticks in the mind.) I remember, too, a friend telling me of going to fetch the body of a mutual friend of ours after he was killed in a car wreck in Mexico. He arrived at the police station to be told the body was in a room out back. As indeed it was: lying in a pool of congealed blood on a concrete floor swarming with flies.

So one is grateful for the antiseptic plainness of Leo P. Gallagher and for soft-spoken Chris.

We sat around the conference table, surrounded by wall displays of headstones, coffins, urns, and reliquary keepsakes—you can put some of the loved one's ashes in a pendant and wear it around your neck, making for one heck of a conversation starter on a first date. As Chris gently slid a piece of paper toward us, I thought of Jessica Mitford's book *The American Way of Death*, published in 1963, coincidentally the year of America's most indelible death. The paper was the price list. Chris said, somewhere between earnest and apologetic, *"Because* our industry is so heavily regulated, that's why all these charges are explained in such detail." So . . . "Basic professional service fee: $2,795." What does that buy you? Don't ask. "Care and prep of remains: refrigeration: $600." Hm. Okay . . . "Transferring remains to funeral home: $695." "Transfer to or from crematory: $395." Wouldn't it just be cheaper to hire a limo? "Brown standard cremation container: $295." Such detail indeed. Well, the industry is so "heavily regulated" in no small part because of Ms. Mitford's exposé. She was, of course, one of the famous five, highly variegated Mitford daughters: Nancy wrote *Love in a Cold Climate*; Diana married British Fascist leader Oswald Mosley, gloriously satirized by P. G. Wodehouse as Sir Roderick Spode, "the amateur dictator" and leader of Britain's Fascist "Black Shorts"; Jessica married an American Communist lawyer with the Dickensian name of Treuhaft and herself made a brilliant success of muckraking journalism, causing vampiric shrieks in U.S. funeral homes coast to coast and, into the bargain, exposing as a money-minting fraud Bennett Cerf's

Famous Writers School. I took a course from her in my senior year at Yale; we cordially loathed each other. But here I found myself her beneficiary, staring at Chris's weirdly detailed price list while scratching my head.

We had come, Pup and I, to arrange for a simple cremation, no frills, the plainest urn—by the end, I was about to suggest that a large Chock full o'Nuts coffee tin would do—but the American Way of Death is, as is the American Way of Life, complicated. I wouldn't have been surprised if, fifteen minutes in, Chris had cleared his throat and said, "Now, would you prefer propane, mesquite, or charcoal briquettes?" I began daydreaming about just bringing dear old Mum home in the back of the car, building a nice roaring bonfire on the beach; but doubtless there's something in the Stamford town code about that.

Buried deep in my Irish DNA is an

atavistic habeas corpus craving for the body. The wake thing. Cremation nullifies that, even if the act of scattering ashes can be ritualistically clean and satisfying. One wants—or I do, anyway—corporeal presence. I remember reading an account by Ken Kesey, heart-wrenching but entirely dry-eyed, of how he dealt with the body of his son, killed in an accident: They brought him home and handmade a coffin for him and buried him themselves. This need is—manifestly—at the root of the Catholic mass, in which bread and wine is "transubstantiated" into the body and blood of Christ. But Pup was adamant. Her ashes were to go into the sculpted bronze cross in the garden, where his would, in turn, also be placed when his time came.

Chris left the room to go total it all up. You could hear a loud *ka-chinng*. When he returned, it all came, somehow, to $6,007.* What is one supposed to say? *Jeez Louise, we're looking for a little cremation, not a full-blown Viking funeral.* Where is Jessica Mitford when you need her?

---

*In the summer of 2008, while revising this book, my friend Rust Hills, the writer and editor, died in Belfast, Maine. I accompanied his widow to the funeral home there to make arrangements. Total cost of cremating Rust: $800. There was no list of "heavily regulated" itemizations. Amusing or . . . outrageous? Why should it cost almost ten times more to cremate someone in suburban Connecticut than it does in coastal Maine? I called my wife after and said, "When I start to fail, get me to Belfast."

CHAPTER 4

That Sounded Like
a Fun Dinner

Pup arranged with the pastor to hold a private service at St. Andrew's, the Episcopalian—or, as my Canadian-born Mum always insisted on calling it, Anglican—church in Stamford. We gathered there Wednesday morning: Pup, me, Danny, Mum's devoted friend

Richard Heanue, and the household staff.

St. Andrew's, it was obvious, had fallen into decay. The stained-glass rosette window above the entrance had been removed. The rectory next door was all boarded up. Perhaps it was because there were only ten of us, in a church built for four hundred or more, but there was a palpable sense of encroaching desolation. It made me sad on this gray and chilly April day to think that a part of Mum's Stamford was passing away along with her.

She was here with us, by the altar, in a neatly wrapped box. Her priest was quite elderly now, semiretired, birdlike, frail but irrepressibly chatty and ebullient, and proud of the homily that he had prepared. He delivered it in singsong tones, indistinguishable from his conversation. I was impressed, yet again, by the superiority of the *Book of Common Prayer* to the pasteurized blancmange of the modern Catholic liturgy. Listening to a contemporary American Catholic priest say the mass invariably reminds me of Robert Taylor as the Roman centurion in *Quo Vadis*, giving himself a salutary whack across the leather breastplate and saying in his Nebraskan accent, *Hail, Marcus Glaucus. By Jupiter, what are they feeding those gladiators at the Colosseum these days?* It just sounds better in the original Latin.

We thanked dear, sweet old Father Flutie. As we left, one of Chris's funeral directors, a lady dressed in a pinstripe pantsuit, handed me my mother in a shopping bag. There was an undeniable symmetry to it: How many shopping bags had I seen Mum toting during her lifetime? Hundreds, anyway. I got into the car and handed the box to Sineda and Julia, Mum's maids, saying—trying to lighten the mood—*"Toma la señora."* (Here, take the señora.) At this they both burst into tears, these dear, devoted, faithful ladies who had taken such loving care of her over the years. They caressed and patted the box lovingly, murmuring to her as we drove back to the house.

Pup announced to me after lunch that we must catalog Mum's books in her bedroom. I was a bit nonplussed. Mum's library would not be mistaken for an annex of the Library of Congress, consisting as it did of a pile of (largely unread) mystery novels and thrillers. I was tired and chafed at this pointless forced labor, but sensing that Pup wanted to keep busy—*industry is the enemy of melancholy*—I went along, duly taking dictation from him on my laptop as he read off the titles. That done, we set down to the more plausible task of going through her papers.

Mum had lost all interest in deskwork during the six or seven months of her invalidity. We found unpaid Gristede's bills, Amex bills; undistributed cash for staff Christmas tips; uncashed checks; unopened letters, including, I saw to my disconcertment, a number from me. This was not carelessness on her part or any failure of affection, but rather fear, and realizing it made me wince in self-rebuke.

Mum's serial misbehavior over the years had driven me, despairing, to write her scolding—occasionally scalding—letters. Now I saw that she'd stopped opening most letters from me, against the possibility that they might contain another excoriation. I opened one of them and read:

Dear Mum,
    That really was an appalling scene at dinner last night. . . .

I wish, now, that I could take back that letter, even though every word of it had been carefully weighed and justified. But looking back, I see it wasn't fair. I'm a professional writer; she was not. So it wasn't a level playing field, however outrageous the provocations that had driven me, hot-faced, flushing, furious, to the keyboard. And they never—ever!—did a bit of good, these pastoral letters of mine. Why, I wondered now, had I never accepted the futility of hurling myself against Fortress Mum? My only consolation was that I had, finally, stopped sending them after our last battle, the previous June. Just as I had exhausted myself in religious warfare with Pup, so had I given up lobbing feckless, well-worded catapult balls over Mum's parapets. I had even refrained from saying anything to her after the last great provocation.

A year earlier, my daughter, Caitlin (Mum's only granddaughter, whom she had more or less lovingly ignored for nineteen years), had gone out to Stamford from New York for the night, bringing with her her best friend, Kate Kennedy. (I know; but there is simply no way to tell this story without using real names.) Cat and Kate look like Irish twin sisters and have been soul-mates since kindergarten. Kate is beautiful, vivacious, bright, witty, and *naughty*—a Kennedy through and through, nicknamed "Kick" after her great-aunt. The friendship between these two colleens is perhaps out of the ordinary given that their paternal grandfathers, Robert F. Kennedy and William F. Buckley Jr., were, shall we say, on somewhat opposite sides of the old political spectrum. At any rate, here were two enchanting young ladies at a grandparental country manse of a summer night. An occasion for joy, affection, delighted conversation. One might . . . sigh . . . think, anyway. I was not—praise the gods—in attendance. Mum and I were not speaking at the time, owing to a prior disgrace of hers, a real beaut even by her standards.

The general mood at the dinner

table that night was not leavened by the continued—indeed, persistent—presence of a British aristocrat lady friend of Mum's who had arrived for a visit ten days before. Now, nearly a fortnight into her encampment at Wallack's Point, she showed no signs of moving on. Pup's graciousness as a host was legendary, but it had limits. The poor man was reduced to sullen japery. *So, A_____, you must be getting jolly homesick for Merry Olde England by now, surely, eh? Ho ho ho. . . .* But Lady A_____ showed no sign of homesickness for Old Blighty. Indeed, she had fastened on to our house with the tenacity of a monomaniacal abalone. Now, on day ten of Pup Held Hostage, his own mood had congealed from sullenness to simmering resentment. Meanwhile, Mum's protracted, vinous afternoons of gin rummy with Her Ladyship had her, by dinnertime, in what might be called the spring-loaded position. In such moods, Mum was capable of wheeling on, say, Neil Armstrong to inform him that he knew nothing—*nothing whatsoever*—about astrophysics or lunar landing. No one in the history of hostessing has ever set a better dinner table than my Mum, but on such evenings, I would rather have supped with al-Qaeda in a guano-strewn cave.

At some point, Mum turned to—*on*, might be the more appropriate preposition—young Kate, informing her that she (Mum) had been an alternate juror in the murder trial of Kate's father's first cousin Michael Skakel. Skakel, nephew of Ethel Kennedy, Kate's grandmother, had (as you are no doubt well aware) been the defendant in a sensational murder trial in Stamford several years before, for the death of fifteen-year-old Martha Moxley back in 1975. Having presented this astonishing (and utterly untrue) credential, Mum then proceeded to launch into a protracted lecture on the villainy of Kate's near relative.

Leave aside the issue of Mr. Skakel's culpability, for which he is, at any rate, currently serving out a twenty-years-to-life sentence. Over the years, I had heard Mum utter whoppers that would make Pinocchio look button-nosed, but this one really took the prize, in several categories, the first being Manners. Why—on earth—would one inflict a jeremiad on an innocent nineteen-year-old girl, one's own grand-daughter's best friend into the bargain? The mind—as Mum herself used to put it—boggles.

This supper table Sturm und Drang I learned about over the phone, from breathless, reeling Cat and Kate once they had reached the sanctu-ary of the pool after dinner, along with a much-needed bottle of wine. All I could say to poor Kate was a stuttery WASP variation on *Oy vey*, along with a candid expostulation: *I am* sooooo *glad not to have been there.* By the time I put down the phone, my blood had reached Fahrenheit 451, the temperature at which it begins to spurt out your ears.

The good news was that I wasn't speaking to Mum at the time, so it seemed pointless to haul out the inkwell, sharpen a quill, and let fly with another well-crafted verbal bitch slapping. Instead, I breathed into a paper bag for a few hours and then called Pup. *Well,* I said, *that sounded like a fun dinner. Sorry to miss it.* He feigned ignorance of the Skakel episode; perhaps he had excused himself early and gone upstairs to short-sheet Lady A_____'s bed. He was, anyway, past caring at this, my five hundredth Howl about Mum's behavior. He tried to wave it away with a spuriously subjunctive, "But why would she say something like that if she *wasn't* a juror at the trial?"

(Pup would have made a superb defense attorney) and changed the subject back to what kinds of explosives work best for dislodging aristocratic British houseguest-limpets. At any rate, it was one letter from me Mum never had to not open. What, really, would have been the point of writing?

I forgive you. I was glad now to have had the chance to say that to her at the hospital, holding her hand, tears streaming down my face. As I type this, I can hear her saying, *Are you* quite *finished? Or shall I go and get my Stradivarius?*

I was five or six years old when I first caught Mum in some preposterous untruth, as she called it. It, too, featured British aristos.

She'd grown up a debutante in a grand house in Vancouver, British Columbia, the kind of house that even has a name: "Shannon." Grand, but Vancouver grand, which is to say, provincial.

Mum's mother had been the daughter of the Winnipeg chief of police; her father, my grandfather, Austin Taylor, was a self-made industrialist (lumber, gold, ranching). His idea of fine art was an oil painting of a quail being retrieved by an English setter. But gosh, it was a glorious place, Shannon: a Georgian mansion surrounded by ten acres of English gardens, walled off from the city around it. It turns up as a movie set (*Carnal Knowledge, Best in Show*). Anyway, Mum's parents were socially prominent in old Vancouver.

So one night, age six or so, sitting with the grown-ups at the dinner table, I heard Mum announce that "the king and queen *always* stayed with us when they were in Vancouver." By "king and queen," she meant the parents of the current queen of England. My little antennae went *twing!* I'd never heard my grandparents refer to a royal visit, which is a pretty big deal. I looked at Mum and realized—*twang!*—that she was telling an untruth. A *big* untruth. And I remember thinking in that instant how thrilling and grown-up it must be to say something so *completely* untrue, as opposed to the little amateur fibs I was already practiced at—horrid little apprentice sinner that I was—like the ones about how you'd already said your prayers or washed under the fingernails. Yes, I was *impressed*. This was my introduction to a lifetime of mendacity. I too must learn to say these gorgeous untruths. Imaginary kings and queens would be *my* houseguests when I was older!

When Mum was in full prevarication, Pup would assume an expression somewhere between a Jack Benny stare and the stoic grimace of a thirteenth-century saint being burned alive at the stake. He knew very well that King George VI and Queen Elizabeth did not routinely decamp at Shannon. The funny thing was that he rarely challenged her when she was in the midst of one of her glorious confections. For that matter, no one did. They wouldn't have dared. Mum had a regal way about her that did not brook contradiction. The only time she ever threatened to spank me was when I told her, age seven, in front of others, following one of her more absurd claims, "Oh, come off it!" Her fluent mendacity, combined with adamantine confidence, made her truly indomitable. As awful as it often was, thinking back on it now, I'm filled with a sort of perverse pride in her. She was really, really good at it. She would have made a fantastic spy. She would have made a fantastic *anything*. She was beautiful, theatrical, bright as a diamond, the wittiest woman I have ever known (whatever talent I possess as a "humorist"—dreadful word—I owe to her). She could have done anything; instead, she devoted herself heart, soul, and body to being Mrs. William F. Buckley Jr. (A full-time job.)

I learned something about her that I had *not* known before, from the *New York Times* obituary—namely, that I owe my very existence to her inability with . . . math. The reason she had gone off to Vassar, an American college three thousand miles away, and where she roomed freshman year with my father's sister Patricia—was that Canadian colleges required a level of math proficiency that eluded her. I don't recall her ever mentioning this fact.

She never finished Vassar. Pup and I heard her give various reasons for this over the years: She had to return to Vancouver because her mother had broken her back while riding; because her brother Firpo had broken his back riding; because *she* had broken her back riding. One night, after imbibing about two acres' worth of vineyard grapes, she informed Pup and me—us!—that she had, in fact, left Vassar "to go back to Vancouver and save my parents' marriage." This revelation was as rococo as it was flabbergasting.

What made it rococo was that she thought to tell it to an audience consisting of 1) her husband, and 2) her son—that is, the two people on earth who knew her best. One might suppose this would obviate the necessity for recreational prevarication. Oh well. Afterward, sitting in the basement sauna, Pup mused aloud, "That makes reason number eight I've heard for her dropping out of Vassar."

Whatever the real reason was—probably nothing much more than ennui with academics—her cap-and-gownless departure from Poughkeepsie left her, for the rest of her life, with a deep-seated insecurity that manifested itself aggressively, especially after the supernumerary glass of wine. On those occasions, more than one of my friends—by whom she was generally adored and whose adoration she returned—might be submitted to cross-examinations on the order of: *So, you're the world's expert on feldspar, are you? Well, doubtless, then, you're aware that 86.5 percent*—how I marveled at the precision of her fabrications—*of the world's supply of feldspar comes from Baffin Island. So what do you have to say to that, Mr. Expert?* The friend in question being a Yale mineralogy PhD was, nonetheless, left to splutter incoherently and beat a quick twitchy retreat in the direction of his borscht.

Pup remarked to me after she died that he had not once, in fifty-seven years, seen her read a nonfiction book. This *did* surprise me. Greatly. She was, after all, a woman who as William F. Buckley's wife spent a great lot of time in the company of intellectual bigfeet—John Kenneth Galbraith, Henry Kissinger, Tom Wolfe, James Burnham, Malcolm Muggeridge, Norman Mailer, Russell Kirk, Enoch Powell, Margaret Thatcher, Norman Podhoretz . . . you name 'em, she fed 'em.

Every one of these people was enchanted by her razor-sharp wit and natural intelligence. Mailer used to call her "Slugger." She may not have spent a lot of time with her nose in biography and history, but she always read the paper thoroughly and kept up with the news on the telly. I remember one Sunday morning being stunned on picking up the *Sunday Times* magazine and seeing that she'd filled the entire crossword puzzle—a feat normally well beyond my own modest abilities. And yet, she might proclaim at the table with an exasperated air, "I simply don't understand why the president just doesn't pass the bloody bill *himself*," leaving it to Pup, slightly embarrassed and sotto voce, to point out to her that passing bills was the province of the legislative and not the executive branch. In my mind, remembering this moment, I hear her coming back with, "Well, if you ask me, it's all *too* ridiculous for words," which is why everyone adored her.

CHAPTER 5

I Don't Want Champagne

❦

By the Friday after she died, I found myself in the kitchen, blurting to poor Julian, "Jules, if I don't get out of here soon, there's going to be another funeral in this house."

Julian Booth (to whom this book is in part dedicated) is the kind, gentle, omnicompetent Briton who had been with my parents almost thirty years as cook and house manager. The nickname "Jules" was bestowed on him by David Niven. Jules nodded through his thick glasses and said quietly, "Yes, Christopher." He is so even-keeled and sweet-tempered that he'd have responded exactly as he did if I'd said to him, "Jules, I am going to detonate a fifty-megaton nuclear device and destroy all life on planet Earth and usher in nuclear winter for a thousand years." *Yes, Christopher.*

A week after Mum's death, the novelty—if that's the right word—of it had worn off. Pup and I had run out of books to catalog, papers to sort. Now there was the matter of Mum's memorial service, and over this we clashed, filling the dining room with the sound of dueling antlers.

But Pup, the New York apartment can only hold, what, eighty, ninety people? How can we possibly hold the reception there? There are going to be hundreds *of people at this thing. Mum was—*

They don't all have to come in at once.

[Sighing.] But we can't have people standing in line *out on 73rd Street, for heaven's sake.*

Let me think about it.

This was WFB code for: I've made up my mind. Discussion over.

Well, let's at least do it right, wherever we hold it. Serve champagne and—

I don't want champagne.

But Mum—

I don't like champagne.

[Sighing.] Okay, but let's at least have nice *wine.*

I have nice *wine.*

Arguable Pup had a fetish about not paying more than eight or nine bucks a bottle, a practice that, though economically sound, did not always result in wine of lip-smacking quality.*

Two cases should do.

[*Spluttering.*] *Two* cases? *For . . . five hundred people?*

People don't drink much, anyway.

By the end of lunch, my fingers were wrapping around the fruit knife in a patricidal grip. It had been a long week. I'd been attentively filial 24/7 to an old, ailing, heartsick (and somewhat high-maintenance) father. Now I was furious over what I perceived as petulant small-mindedness.

For over a half century of unstinting

---

*This fetish could be carried to sometimes hurtful extremes. On his seventy-fifth birthday, I presented him with a trophy case of wine. In front of everyone at the table, he grimaced and said: "How much was this?" I demurred, saying, "It's nice wine, Pup. Happy birthday." "I asked you how much was it?" "About seventy dollars a bottle." "Take it back. I wouldn't enjoy it." Happy birthday!

and heroic (if not quite uncomplaining) effort, Mum had made my father's various households—in Stamford, New York, and Switzerland—paradigms of hospitality. She was (I boast) a great, even grand, hostess. The food, the decor, the service, *everything* was impeccability and perfection. You don't have to take my word for it: Pat Buckley was acknowledged universally as one of the great ladies of New York, and all this she accomplished without the kind of bank account most other New York great hostesses tend to have.* But they lived well—very well—if always with a sharp eye to

---

*My parents were wealthy by any standard, but not (as Mum used to put it) "rich-rich." Pup had lost his entire patrimony in the stock market by the mid-1950s; every penny thereafter he earned the old-fashioned way, through ceaseless lectures, fifty-five books, TV, his syndicated column. Mum inherited a yearly income from her father's estate in the mid-1960s, but it was not nearly sufficient to sustain their lifestyle.

the marginal expense; whence Pup's borderline Scrooginess in the matter of the household grape. But now I simmered. Here she had put on the show for him for fifty-seven years, and here I was trying to wheedle an extra case or two of indifferent plonk with which to refresh five hundred or more attendees at her memorial service, the majority of whom he seemed perfectly content to let cool their heels out on the sidewalk. It was—too much. Or as Mum would have said, *beyond comprehension.*

"I'm going to kill him," I said to Danny, escalating from my statement to Julian.

"I think you need to get out of here," he said. Danny has been exquisitely attuned to our family reverberations since about 1965.

This I did. The next morning, safe in my New York apartment, I tapped out a come-to-Jesus e-mail to him.

Pup and I had been going at it with the

verbal light-sabers—*vwhum vwhum-mmm*—since about 1966, when I was shipped off to the monks at Portsmouth Abbey. Pup never really, ever, yielded an inch of ground. That was his victory. I ended up with a sharp sword and an attitude; that was mine. I don't mean to make it sound as though I grew up in ancient Sparta; Pup and I exchanged, over the course of a lifetime, letters of deep and abundant affection. But we fought, and hard. Of the perhaps—I'm guessing—seven thousand or so letters and e-mails we exchanged, I'd estimate that one-half were contentious. A lot of it was due to his having, about the early 1970s, turned me into a de facto marriage counselor—something I would strenuously urge any parent against.

I wrote:

Dear Pup,

I don't right now have the emotional reserves to argue with you over this.

Suffice to say it wounds me when you bark at me, after a rather trying week in which I was Cordelian in my filiality, "I don't want champagne," when Mum, who devoted her life to making your homes paradigms of resplendent hospitality, drowned thousands of your guests in it, to say nothing of stuffing them cross-eyed with caviar and every conceiveable sweetmeat. And if pari passu—as you might put it—you're determined to hold a reception for 500 guests in a space that at best holds 80, I don't have it in me to argue about that, either, but it seems to me a very queer way to memorialize one of New York's great hostesses. But why don't I step aside and let you arrange all that as well. So over to you.

Love, Christo

I counted to ten—I've learned *that* much over a lifetime—and hit send. His reply came back. (I've cleaned up the typos.) *Dear Christo, Am absolutely astonished by what you say and have no memory of it. xxP*

This wasn't a disingenuous response, but neither did it move the ball down the field. At times I had to remind myself, by way of autoconsolation, that I was dealing with William F. Buckley Jr., the legendary host of *Firing Line*, one of the great debaters of the twentieth century. He had not made his name for himself by yielding on the field of battle. In this contest I was a chipmunk pitted against a rhino. I decided to let things cool for a day or so. Pup was not adept at the cooling-off and the next day fired back with: *You've picked one hell of a time to abandon your father.* My fingers hovered above the Launch Missile button on the laptop, but I refrained. The chipmunk, confronting force majeure, does what the chipmunk must— and calls Aunt Pitts.

If there was a single human being

on the planet who exercised anything like authority over William F. Buckley Jr., it was his older sister Priscilla, now eighty-six. She had been, for about a half century, managing editor of *National Review* and in that capacity was a beloved den- and godmother to generations—literally—of intellectual writer talent, from Garry Wills to George Will; to say nothing of being a cherished aunt and surrogate mother to fifty nieces and nephews, a number of them orphaned.* I said to her, *Pitts—do something.*

Pitts called back within the hour and said, *It's done.*

As the saying goes, *Be careful what you pray for, you might just get it.* I now found myself with carte blanche,

———

*Pitts was the only one of ten Buckley children not to marry and have children, yet I think in some ways she had more children than all her siblings put together.

in charge of Pat Buckley's memorial service. This would take a month.

I TURNED, FIRST, to one of Mum's great New York friends. It may not come as a huge surprise when I reveal that her closest friends were, by and large, gay gentlemen. Pup was once asked in a published interview if he was aware of the statistical datum that roughly 10 percent of the U.S. male population is homosexual. He replied, "If that's the case, then I've met them all." I did, too, starting in the 1950s when they were known as "confirmed bach-elors." They adored Mum and she them. Some of them didn't bother to hang around inside the closet, even in those homophobic days. One of them was Christopher Hewett, exquisitely memorable as the flamboyantly homo director Roger De Bris in the origi-nal movie *The Producers*. One weekend at Stamford, he participated in a sixteen-millimeter silent home movie we shot called *Anesthesia*. (The dialogue appeared between scenes, written on a blackboard.) Christopher played—it goes without saying—the grand duchess Anesthesia. Pup, wearing a plastic skullcap, played a Bolshevik (the only time WFB essayed a Commie role); Mum was a glamorous, chain-smoking revolutionary named (as I recall) Natasha. I played, appropriately enough, the imbecile six-year-old heir to the Russian throne. The climactic moment comes when Pup, in disguise as a servant in the royal household, is asked by the grand duchess to "toss the salad." Being a peasant, Pup misinterprets this as an instruction to reach into the salad bowl and start throwing lettuce at the various guests. That was a fun weekend. I earned a whole dollar for my day's work as an actor.

In the 1960s, the term *walker* entered the language—that is to say, the society column newspaper word for a gentleman who escorts the wives of famous busy men to Broadway first nights and balls and such. Mum's great friend Jerome Zipkin was the walker of record in those days. His most famous walkee was Nancy Reagan. When she became the nation's first lady in 1981, various liberal publications had a tricky time squaring their attempts to make her out to be a reincarnation of Marie Antoinette, with their vaunted tolerance of homosexuality. (Zip, wearing his trademark homburg hat and fur-lined collar, just stuck his tongue out at them, and bravo, Jerome. I was very fond of him and sad when the falling-out came between him and Mum. He had a bit of a mean streak, and she had a low tolerance for mean streaks.) Another of Mum's very close friends was Conservative Party appa-

ratchik Marvin Liebman, a confirmed
bachelor until he spilled a very large
can of beans in the form of a memoir entitled *Coming Out Conservative*.* There were so many of them: Bill
Blass, Peter Glenville, Valentino, John
Richardson, Truman Capote, and others who prefer still to be thought of as
confirmed bachelors. At this pageant,
I had a front-row seat. And though this
may verge on truism or overstatement,
I grasped, at perhaps a precocious
age, that no one truly appreciates a really great lady more than a gay man,
and vice versa. Whether this mutual
valence is organically due to the lib-
erating lack of sexual interest in each
other or to shared passions (decor,

---

*It's interesting, in retrospect, how many Republican
and conservative operatives/figures were gay—
Marvin, Terry Dolan, Arthur Finkelstein, Roy Cohn,
Bob Bauman—almost all of them distinguished by an
aggressive, one might even say combative, style.

food, dress, whatever; Truman Capote and Babe Paley reportedly used to discuss moisturizers in Talmudic detail), I don't know, and don't propose here to essay a half-baked master's thesis on the subject. In Mum's case, it seemed to have more to do with laughter than moisturizers. At any rate, after a half century of hanging around Mum and her pals, I knew where to look. Having exhausted various Protestant venues up and down the silky Rialto of Madison Avenue, I placed a hopeful call to the Metropolitan Museum's Costume Institute, whose annual galas Mum had administered for over a decade, and was generously offered the Temple of Dendur, which is roughly speaking the coolest space on the planet.

"How did you manage to get the Temple of Dendur?" Pup said excitedly over the phone.

"Oh," I said, "I have my ways, you know," though it had absolutely nothing to do with my powers of persuasion. Mum had made the Costume Institute hot, and now they were returning the favor.

CHAPTER 6

Dude, What's With Your Dad?

❧

A Celebration of the Life of
PATRICIA TAYLOR BUCKLEY
July 1, 1926–April 15, 2007

The Metropolitan Museum of Art
May 14, 2007

Isuppose one way or the other I've spent a good deal of my life, despite my protestations to the contrary, trying to measure up to my father, so it was refreshing—or novel, anyway—to find myself now trying to measure up to my mother, by throwing her a worthy memorial service.

There was a lot to do: designing the program, arranging with caterers, florists, the audiovisual guy, preparing a PowerPoint presentation, lining up eulogists, making sure the invitations got out. I was a novice in this field of endeavor, but I now feel that I could with confidence arrange a wedding or, for that matter, a state visit by the queen of England. (Did I mention that the queen's father and mother used to stay with us whenever they were in town?)

With the food and booze and the flowers, all I needed to say to Mum's old friend Sean Driscoll of Glorious Food was: What would Pat do? Sean got it; that was all the guidance he needed. The audiovisual subcontractor, a competent and agreeable man named Tony, presented his estimate. I whistled silently at the $7,000 price at the bottom of the e-mail, but I thought, *Well, we're only going to do this once.* A month later, my learning curve took a sharp turn upward when Tony presented his final bill and I realized that I hadn't read quite all the way to the bottom of his e-mail attachment. The $7,000 was for equipment. The *labor* cost came to an additional $13,000 on top of that. As I type this a year later, I'm able to chuckle—finally—at my ineptitude at e-mail attachment reading. I can hear Mum's ghost muttering, *Twenty* thousand *dollars? For a few television screens and a microphone? Have you* completely *taken leave of your senses?*

That said, I think she would have approved of the reason I needed eight humongous plasma-screen TV monitors placed about the Temple of Dendur. They were to display the opening and closing PowerPoint presentation (what we used to call in the old days a "slide show"), consisting of a photo-montage set to Michael Feinstein's "Isn't It

Romantic?" and "Where Do You Start?" Preparing these photos had occupied several full days of standing over them spread across the living room floor, arranging them and timing the music, the whole time sobbing. (This presented a deplorable spectacle for my son, Conor, and his fifteen-year-old pals as they traipsed in and out of the room. *Dude, what's with your dad? Is he like a total retard or something?*) But I couldn't help it. She was so, so beautiful, Mum. Among those hundreds of photos, there wasn't one bad one. She made love to every camera that came her way. Well, it was probably good therapy in the end. By the morning of the memorial service, I had—quite literally—cried myself dry.

Some people, no matter how dear and good their hearts, just aren't adept at eulogies; still, they have to be asked to give them. This presents the memorial service impresario with a conundrum:

how to square his obligation to the bereaved with the dramatic requirements of the service. And this can be tricky.

One of the people I asked to give one—a longtime friend of Mum's—said he would be honored to do so, then phoned me a day or two later to ask a bit sheepishly if I might provide "a few notes" to help him. I sensed this might be code for "Could you write it for me?" I was happy to oblige.

I'd asked my daughter, Caitlin, if she might speak. Cat was nineteen and in the throes of approaching final exams, and very pressed for time, so I volunteered to do some talking points for her. I sat down during a train ride to sketch these out and found myself quickly and utterly stymied. I couldn't think of a single warm and fuzzy grandmother anecdote. (The Skakel story, warm and fuzzy as it was, might—I felt—not be quite appropriate to the occasion.) I phoned Cat from the train and with genuine pain in my heart said, *Honey, you don't have to do this. She loved you in her own way, but let's face it— she was not a hands-on granny.* Dear, sweet Cat said, *No, no, Dad, I want to do it.* This somehow liberated me, and I was able to give her some ideas, the gist of which was that while "Nan" may not have been a typical grandmother, she was never (God knows) dull. She had taught Cat such useful skills as never buttering your bread in midair; taught her, age four, to air kiss, telling her that this would come in handy when she grew up and moved to New York City. Cat's eulogy ended up being the high point of the entire show. She ended it with blowing an air kiss to her Nan. It was a total home run. I did little after the service other than kvell and accept compliments on behalf of my dazzling daughter. Anna Wintour of *Vogue* was so impressed, she offered Cat a job. This was very generous of Ms. Wintour and presented Cat with an interesting dilemma inasmuch as *The Devil Wears Prada* had just opened.

Neither Pup nor I trusted ourselves to get through a eulogy. He wrote one for the program. Mine took the form of the memorial service itself, along with my weepy PowerPoint show.

The key to eulogist wrangling—bear this in mind when you find yourself doing it—is *Draconian enforcement of the time limit!* In fact, to heck with Draco: Imagine yourself as the Time-Limit Nazi. This may seem an obvious point, but you've probably attended one or two funerals and memorial services where the fine-hammered steel of woe was turned to Brillo by incontinent eulogists. This species can be easily spotted: They almost never prepare ahead of time, preferring instead to "go with the moment" or to "speak from the heart." They will then prattle on—from the heart—for at least twenty minutes, causing those in attendance to forget all about the deceased and start praying that a dislodged gargoyle will fall from above and smite the speaker.[*]

A twenty-minute eulogy, unless composed by a) William Shakespeare, b) Winston Churchill, or c) Mark Twain, is sixteen minutes too long. Technical note: It is better to tell a eulogist to speak for four minutes, not five minutes. "Five minutes" to the modern ear sounds like "around five minutes," whereas "four minutes" means "four minutes." Just before the service began, I said to my eulogists (including Henry Kissinger), "I have snipers positioned up there"—

---

[*]An inspired eulogy, on the other hand, can be a transcendental experience. The "Funeral Blues" recitation in *Four Weddings and a Funeral* ("He was my North, my South, my East and West") created a W. H. Auden revival and a spike in sales of the poet's anthologies. Come to think of it, arguably the most famous soliloquy in all Shakespeare is a eulogy beginning "Friends, Romans, countrymen ..."

pointing to the temple—"with orders to shoot to kill anyone who goes over four minutes." I smiled as I said this, but smiled in a certain way. And it worked. They were all splendid, moving, and brief. No one went beyond his or her allotted time—except for the Catholic padre (Pup had insisted on him) who gave the opening benediction. It was brilliant, subtle, amusing, intellectually elegant, and seven minutes long.

So it all went very well and was worthy of Pat Buckley. And it had taken a month to arrange. When on that May morning I walked into the sunlit Temple of Dendur—a two-thousand-year-old Nubian temple to the goddess Isis, enclosed within a vast, stippled glass atrium and reflecting pool—and saw the huge spray of pink apple blossoms, the chairs smartly lined up, my programs, Tony's $20,000 worth of TV screens and technical people, saw the dozens of Sean Driscoll's smartly attired catering staff, I took it all in and gave myself a little pat on the back and thought, *Yes, Mum would approve.*

Pup arrived as I was having this quiet little moment of self-congratulation. I winked at him and spread my arms as if to say, *So—whaddya think?* He looked about the room and grimaced. "It's awfully *bright*, isn't it?" He was used to seeing it at night, during Mum's Costume Institute galas. I suppressed the urge to hurl him into the reflecting pool. After it was over, I looked over and saw him lurching on unsteady legs to embrace Henry Kissinger. Poor Pup, poor desolate man—his face was flushed, livid, scarlet with grief. This is the eulogy from the program that he couldn't bring himself to deliver a cappella in the shadow of the old Egyptian goddess:

By any standard, at near six feet tall, she was extraordinary. She shared a suite with my sister

Trish and two other students at Vassar, and on that spring evening in 1949 I was the blind date she had never met. When I walked into the drawing room the four girls shared, I found her hard pressed. She was mostly ready for the prom but was now vexed by attendant responsibilities. I offered to paint her fingernails, and she immediately extended her hand, using the other one on the telephone. The day before, she had given the sad news to her roommates that she would not be returning to Vassar for junior and senior years. She was needed at home, in Vancouver, to help her mother care for a dying family member. My own parents had gone to their place in South Carolina for the winter and the house in Sharon, Connecticut, was closed. But I would dart over from Yale for an occasional weekend in the huge empty house, and Trish brought her there once, and we laughed all weekend long, and Trish promised to visit her in Vancouver during the summer.

I had a summer job in Calgary working for my father in the oil business, and from there happily flew over to Vancouver to join Trish and Pat for a weekend. Her father's vast house occupied an entire city block, but did not dampen our spirits. On the contrary, the tempo of our congeniality heightened, and on the third day I asked if she would marry me. She rushed upstairs to tell her mother, and I waited at the bottom of the huge staircase hoping to get the temper of her proud mother's reaction (her father was out of town), and soon I heard peals of laughter. I waited apprehensively for Pat to advise me what that was all about. The laughter, she revealed, was generated by her mother's taking the occasion to recall that eight times in the past, Pat had reported her betrothal.

One year later, in the company of about a thousand guests, we exchanged vows. Two months after that, we rented a modest house in the neighborhood of New Haven. Pat resolved to learn how to cook. Her taste was advanced and her ambitions exigent, so she commuted to New York City and learned cooking from experts, becoming one herself. Meanwhile, I taught a class in Spanish to undergraduates and wrote God and Man at Yale.

Primarily to avoid exposure to further duty as an infantry officer, I joined the CIA and we went to live in Mexico City, buying and decorating a lovely house at San Angel Inn. Pat was radiant and hyperactive in maintaining the house and its little garden. She resolutely failed to learn the language, even though, until the end, the staff was Spanish-speaking, but intercommunication was electrically effective.

Her solicitude was such that she opposed any venture by me which she thought might adversely affect me. She opposed the founding of National Review, my signing up with a lecture agency, my non-fiction books and then my fiction books, my contract to write a weekly column, the projected winter in Switzerland, my decision to run for mayor of New York. Yet once these enterprises were undertaken, she participated enthusiastically. It was she *who located the exquisite house, every inch of which she decorated, that we shared for 55 years. We had only one child, Christopher, of whom she was understandably proud. And it was she—all but uniquely she—who brought here the legion of guests, of all ages, professions, and interests, whose company made up her lively life.*

Her infirmities dated back to a skiing accident in 1965. She went through four hip replacements over the years. She went into the hospital a fortnight ago, but there was no thought of any terminal problem. Yet following an infection, on the seventh day, she died, in the arms of her son.

Friends from everywhere were quick to record their grief. One of them* was especially expressive. "Allow a mere acquaintance of your wife to sense the magni-

tude of your loss. As surely as she physically towered over her surroundings, she must have mentally, spiritually, and luminously surpassed ordinary mortals. She certainly was in every sense of the term une grande dame, a distinction she wore as lightly as a T-shirt—not that one can imagine her in anything so plebeian. The only consolation one may offer is that the greatness of a loss is the measure of its antecedent gain. And perhaps also that Pat's memory will be second only to her presence. For as long as you live, people will share with you happy reminiscences that, in their profusion, you may have forgotten or not even known.

"I am a confirmed nonbeliever,

---

*John Simon, the theater critic and author.

but for once I would like to be mistaken, and hope that, for you, this is not good-bye, but hasta luego."

No alternative thought would make continuing in life, for me, tolerable.

—WFB

CHAPTER 7

You Need to Get Here as Quickly as You Can

By the end of May, I was in ragged shape. Mum's death had come after long months of her final illness, which takes a toll on those attending the sickbed. She died as I was two weeks into a busy book launch tour that itself had come on the heels of a busy lecture tour.

I had my day job as editor of *ForbesLife* magazine in New York and had begun work on a new novel. Meanwhile Pup, his health increasingly fragile, required more of my attention. At such times, the only child begins to yearn for an older sister to whom he can say, *I'm outta here.* You *deal with it.*

Whatever. I was tired, terribly out of shape physically and emotionally, so I went off by myself to Zermatt, Switzerland, for a week of hiking, sensible eating, book work, and general resetting of the old circuit breakers. I took along a promising new book by Alexander Waugh, grandson of Evelyn and son of Auberon, called *Fathers and Sons.* In the mornings I worked on my novel in bed while looking out the window at the Matterhorn, quite the most amazing vista in the world; afternoons I hauled my adipose carcass up and down various mountainsides, then swam in the hotel pool, took a steam, had a cocktail in my room as I did e-mail, ate an early scrumptious Swiss dinner, got into bed with Mr. Waugh's superb book about being the grandson and son of famous writers, and was asleep by nine to the sound of the river rushing past outside. Just what the doctor ordered.

Upon arriving at the little hotel the first day, jet-lagged and grimy, I checked my e-mail and found this: *Dear Christo, Jane died. Say a prayer. xxp**

Jane was my aunt, Pup's slightly older sister. She'd been ill for many years with emphysema. Buckleys appear to have a genetic predisposition to this condition: Pup, Jane, and my uncle Reid all got it. Jane in her prime smoked maybe three packs a day. For nearly ten years, she had waged a valiant and uncomplaining battle against the gradual suf-

---

*I've cleaned up the typos once again and will do so with all of them, at least the ones I can decipher.

focation; by the time she died, she was down to something like 4 percent of lung capacity. My uncle Reid, in his nicotinic heyday, had consumed four packs of Kools—Kools! As for Pup, he had sworn off cigarettes at age twenty-seven after one lulu of an Easter Sunday hangover, but he smoked cigars, which—unlike President Clinton—he inhaled, with the dreadful consequence that he now struggled for breath. I have had asthma all my life, which every now and then lands me in the hospital, so I know something of the cold, sweaty, 3 a.m. panic of reaching for a lungful of air that isn't there.

Pup had been in denial about his emphysema for years. Seeing him huff and puff after just a short walk or climbing the stairs, I would say, *Pup, do you think you might have . . . ?* He would wave off the e-word. *No, no. Just a cold.* But it was increasingly obvious, and doubly cruel on top of the sleep apnea he suffered from. Mum, who herself had smoked for sixty-five years—sixty-five!—never pestered him on the subject, I suspect out of superstitition, not wanting to tempt her own fate. Finally Pup hauled himself off to the Mayo Clinic in Rochester, where he got the official news; yet even then he refused to use the word *emphysema*, at least for a time. He'd say, *There's apparently some scar tissue down there from the cigars,* and change the subject.

There was a gloomy irony to his emphysema. In 1967, when I was fifteen and at boarding school, he had sent me a letter. He'd just visited with a cousin of his in Texas who had emphysema. Pup reported its effects in lurid detail: *By the time he has finished going to the bathroom, he no longer has the strength to wipe himself.* As I read, horrified, I recall thinking, *Gee, Pup, thanks for sharing all this.* The letter went on and on; then he got to the point: It had come to his attention that I was smoking cigarettes. *Damn—who told him?* My sixteenth birthday was coming up, and his signature was required to get my driver's license. *Uh-oh. . . .* Said signature would not be forthcoming unless I agreed to give them up. In return, he would give me "anything you ask for." He was always so generous that way. If you met him halfway, he'd meet you all the way. Unless, of course, it was a debate. (Old story.)

I went into a prolonged, furious, impotent, adolescent sulk. Pup's diktaks tended to have that effect on me. Perhaps it was a consequence of our essentially epistolary relationship. But being a devious little shit, I came up with a devilishly clever way of punishing him. *Okay*, I said, *I'll give up smoking. But in return, I want to attend summer school here at Portsmouth so I can take Greek.* Take that! I would deprive him of my company over the summer! Brilliant!

Once the initial thrill of my clever stratagem had worn off, I began to consider the essentially Pyrrhic aspect of my ploy. The idea of staying at boarding school over the summer to study—what was I thinking?—ancient Greek was about as appealing as, I don't know, being handcuffed to a radiator in Beirut by Hezbollah; but my twisted little brain was intent on revenge, and I really had him over a barrel. *He'd promised!*

There followed a fevered volley of transatlantic letters (he was in winter quarters near Gstaad, Switzerland, writing another book). I clung to my position like a limpet. In the end, facing the actual prospect of summer at Portsmouth declining *ho potomo, hou potamou*, I relented. A cautious peace was established. Nothing more was said on the subject of smoking.

Then, years later, poking through his desk drawers in his study in Stamford—don't ask; I've always been a sneaky little bastard—I found a copy of a letter he had written to Father Leo, my headmaster at Portsmouth, inquiring if my inexplicable insistence on attending summer school to learn Greek was due to—as he put it—"an amorous dalliance" (translation: homosexual) with another boy. I was dumbstruck reading this. God only knows what poor old Father Leo must have thought. Had he instigated discreet inquiries among the other monks? *Is young Buckley, um, doing anything . . . out of the normal these days?* I draw from this pathetic tale two lessons: Leave revenge to the professionals, and don't go poking about in other people's correspondence—you might not like what you find.

I continued my idiotic, willful juvenile delinquency and smoked on and off until September 14, 1988, when, after three days at the bedside of a friend dying of lung cancer ("He has twelve tumors in his lungs the size of golf balls," the doctor told us), I simply stopped. It was as if a toggle switch had forever clicked to the off position. Now Pup was writing to tell me that his beloved sister Jane had finally been killed by the cigarettes she'd smoked. As I stared blearily at the e-mail, the awful thought went through my mind that something like this lay in wait for Pup, too.

I loved Jane—everyone did. But I didn't have it in me—this crowded, deathful spring—to turn around and get back on a plane and fly three thousand miles to another funeral. I just didn't. So I e-mailed my love and condolences to Pup and his brothers and sisters—there were ten of them, originally; now six remained—and to my cousins, Jane's six wonderful children. And then unpacked.

A day or so later, there was another e-mail from Pup—they were getting increasingly indecipherable—referring casually (I felt) to the fact that he would miss Jane's funeral because he had to go to Washington, D.C., to accept an award. I thought, *Huh?* It wasn't the Nobel Peace Prize, but some lifetime anticommunism award. (I don't mean any disrespect.) I mused on this as I dragged myself up steep alpine slopes, avoiding sheep dip. I kept thinking, *Pup . . . skipping your sister's funeral? To pick up another award?*

By now, Pup had more awards than have been given out in the entire history of the Olympics; more honorary degrees than Erasmus; more medallions than the entire New York City taxi fleet; more . . . well, you get the point. He'd received about every honor there is, including the Presidential Medal of Freedom and—finally—an honorary degree from Mother Yale. But not to attend Jane's funeral . . . for this? I tried to put it out of my mind. I'd come to the lush Valais and its loamy, ovine pastures to rejuvenate, not recriminate; and I chided myself that, having myself declined the bother of getting on a plane to fly back for the funeral, I was hardly in a position to tsk-tsk. *Still.* A voice within me kept noodging, *Dude—it's your sister's funeral*! I e-mailed him to the effect, *Pup, are you sure about this?* He e-mailed back that he was attending the dinner in Sharon the night before the funeral with all the Buckleys and it was fine that he wouldn't be at the actual funeral. It was a "non-issue." This was one of Pup's favorite practical formulations: *It's a non-issue.*

I shrugged, there being nothing much further to say, and wheezed myself up the next mountainside. On these climbs, I was an object of curiosity to the marmots, who would pop up out of holes and make high-pitched noises at me and then disappear. The sun shone, the sky was cerulean, the air like Perrier. It was glorious.

Pup's e-mails over the following

days became increasingly incoherent, eventually to the point of near complete inscrutability. I e-mailed Danny, who replied that he had returned from Washington "in kind of bad shape" but was "doing better now." I'd be home in three days. Pup and I had dinner planned for the night I got back.

JUST AS I WAS PULLING OFF the Stamford exit on I-95, my cell phone trilled. I was jet-lagged and a bit sticky from the flight. I didn't recognize the number, a 203 area code.

Chris?

Yes?

It's Gavin McLeod, your dad's doctor.

Gavin had never called. No, not a good sign.

Your dad is at the hospital here. He came here by ambulance. We're doing tests. We're not sure what it is, but he really needs to stay here. But he keeps insisting to leave. He says he's having dinner with you tonight.

So it was back to Stamford Hospital. The scene, on my arrival on the fourth floor, was—looking back on it—mildly comical. Gavin had called me again, this time his normally equable voice pitched to a higher octave of urgency: *He's insisting on trying to leave, and . . . you need to get here as quickly as you can.* I reported that I was driving through downtown Stamford as fast as the law would permit. But I did feel Gavin's pain, for when William F. Buckley Jr. "was insisting" on something, attention must be paid.

I arrived on Four South. There, at the end of the hallway, he was: wearing a green-and-white-striped polo shirt and his blue Greek yachting cap, holding a cane and—weirdly—the Alexander Waugh book *Fathers and Sons* that I'd sent him for Father's Day. He was

in a wheelchair and being gently re-
strained from rotating himself down
the hall by 1) Gavin, 2) two nurses,
3) the unit head, 4) the deputy administrator of Stamford Hospital, and 5) a
large black orderly named Maurice.

Gavin, seeing me scurry toward this
mobile levee, looked vastly relieved.
He leaned over and said to Pup in the
singsong child tone that suggests the
listener isn't working off a full mental deck, *Bill—here's Christopher. It's
Christopher. Christopher is here. Isn't
that wonderful?*

CHAPTER 8

We're Terribly Late
as It Is

Pup was smiling. He *was* pleased to see me, and though his love for me was deep and abiding, I knew very well that his maniacal grin might be more eloquent of my utility to him as an escape vehicle than of paternal affection.

I was entirely sympathetic—who wants to stay in the hospital?—but the situation was plain: He was in seriously awful shape. Maurice—sweet, kind Maurice—kept saying, *Mr. Buckley, we're gonna take you back to your room now, okay?* But the Lion of the Right was having none of that. No, no. Pup merely smiled and shook his head at Maurice, declaring firmly, *No! I'm going to have dinner with my son. He's right here. Christo is taking me home. Let's go, Christo.*

Christo looked at Gavin. Gavin looked at Christo. Good, earnest Gavin tried gamely, in his best *Mister Rogers' Neighborhood* voice, to explain to his (im)patient that leaving the hospital was not a viable option. *Bill, we need to monitor your kidneys. Your kidneys.*

Pup grinned his mad grin at him and gently shook his head, as if Gavin were trying to pull a fast one.

Gavin tried again. *There's something going* on *with your* KIDNEYS.

I didn't like the sound of this. It's one thing when doctors talk about the heart. We all know about the heart. It's a pump, basically, and it needs to keep pumping and doing its other hearty-pumpy things. But when doctors start muttering about your kidneys—organs—it has an unsettling sound.

Pup waved away the kidney talk. *No, no, I'm going home.* He grinned triumphantly. *Christo and I have a dinner date! Don't we, Christo?*

Christo had no thought other than to make his beloved Pup happy. At the same time, Christo sensed that wheeling beloved Pup out of the hospital, with half a dozen pairs of hands clinging to the wheelchair, heels making skidmarks in the hall . . . would not an elegant exit make. And what then? Was I to stop at Barnes & Noble on the way home and pick up a copy of *Kidney Failure for Dummies* so I could fix the problem myself?

Pup, I said, *tell you what. Let's get you back into bed, JUST FOR A LITTLE BIT, OKAY? That way Gavin here can sort out what's going on with your* riñones*—

No, no, no! He shook his head, giving the armrest of the wheelchair an emphatic whack with his palm. His grin was now gone, replaced with a look of something like fear. *We're having* dinner. *A lovely dinner. I've arranged it all. . . .*

He was clutching my arm. It wrenched my heart. This was terra nova to me: the delusional parent who must be denied for his own good. Every fiber of one's being reflexively inclines to accede to the wishes of a parent. It is *contra naturam* (to use a WFB term) to say no to someone who has raised you, clothed you, fed you

_____

*Spanish, as you've probably guessed, for kidneys.

from day one—well, even if, in Pup's case, these actual duties were elaborately subcontracted; still, it feels as though you're disobeying and in contravention of the Fourth Commandment. This is the crushing, awful daily lot of the children of Alzheimer's patients. *No, Mom, let's* not *put our fingers in the blender, okay?*

There wasn't anything else to do but give Maurice, our situational Luca Brasi, the go-ahead to get Pup back into bed. It wasn't altogether an easy operation. Pup, superbly slender figured all his life, had in recent years added some avoirdupois—as indeed had I—along with the accompanying complication of diabetes.

Once he was in bed, I stroked his forehead and spoke soothingly of the dinner we would *absolutely, definitely* have just as soon as the doctors figured out the kidney situation. He was babbling now, incoherent. When a Hispanic nurse came to take his vitals, he sang to her in fluent Spanish, which surprised and charmed her. Otherwise, the most articulate man in America was speaking gibberish.

Gavin said he'd give him something "to moderate the agitation level." The nurses injected Ativan (an agitation level moderator) into his IV drip. Gavin and I huddled in the hallway. Pup had come back from the award ceremony trip badly sick; had for several days thrown up, becoming dehydrated, which in turn distressed his kidneys, which in turn took it out on the brain and the heart. I arranged for a cot.

It was a long night, after a long day, which had started in Geneva many time zones away. I did what I could to calm him down, but despite the Ativan he was feverishly agitated and desperate to leave the hospital. He had to catch a train. Had to get on the boat. He was now very late for an important meeting.

When are we leaving? I had to restrain him physically every five minutes. After the fifteenth or twentieth time, one's patience begins to wear. *Pup,* I finally said, my tone stern: *We're staying here, okay?*

No, I'm leaving. Would you get my clothes?

He tried again to get out of bed, a complicated maneuver given the half dozen tubes and monitor wires, to say nothing of the catheter, which if yanked out would have caused excruciating pain and God knows what kind of plumbing damage. I had to wrestle him back into bed, at which point he began to projectile vom— Well, as I said, it was a long night. I pleaded with the nurses for more Ativan, a drug I would come to revere over the next fortnight. Finally, near delirium myself, I sang an Irish song to him that I had heard on my first visit there:

*If you ever go across the sea to
   Ireland,
Be it only at the closing of your
   days,
You can sit and watch the moon
   rise over Claddagh,
And see the sun go down on Gal-
   way Bay.*

It's a sweet, slightly sad melody. He
quieted as I sang.

*That's beautiful, Christo.
Yes, Pup, it is. I first heard it in—
Where are my clothes?
Why do you need your clothes,
Pup?
We have to go.
Pup—
We're terribly late as it is.*

THE NEXT MORNING, early, I was sitting on a stone wall outside the main

entrance to Stamford Hospital, bleary-eyed, texting Lucy.

Handsome, dapper Joe D'Amico, Mum's orthopedist (*She's already in heaven*), walked out briskly and, glancing sideways at me, did a double take.

Chris? What are you— Aw, shit. Bill?

I told him Pup was in room 4109. He said, *Let me see what I can find out.* He came back fifteen minutes later.

I'm not a urologist, but from the numbers, I think he may be on the verge of renal failure.

"Renal failure" is not a phrase to lift the spirits. Joe went off to tend to his patients. I texted: "Poss. Kidney failure." I looked at the words on the little screen and pressed send and realized that I was crying. (Yet again, at Stamford Hospital.)

Pup was a prominent man, and word was soon out that he was in the hospital. The calls started coming in. They were all well-meaning and large-hearted and sincere, but it is exhausting. The consoler is himself seeking to be consoled. By the second day, I was overwhelmed and began sending out daily bulletins by e-mail. If they sound delirious themselves, my defense is that they were written early in the morning, after generally unrestful nights.

For Family and Friends Only, Please
WFB Jr. Medical Bulletin
June 20, 8 am

He has something called "acute tubular necrosis," which sounds pretty dreadful, but there's also good news.

ATN is basically kidney damage caused by, in his case, extreme dehydration and decreased blood flow to the kidneys caused by a drop in heart rate. (His heart rate is now back to normal.)

Basically, his kidneys are damaged and need to get better. The good news is that they regenerate on their own. This can take 1–3 days, or 10 days.

Within a day or two his doctor, a pro's pro named William Hines with a lovely bedside manner, will decide whether to recommend dialysis—as a temporary measure—to stimulate regeneration.

So there we are. We're here at Stamford Hospital for the duration.

He's resting. He wakes up every hour to declare loudly to everyone that he can't sleep and needs "a much *stronger* Ambien." I take this as a good sign that he's quite himself.

I'll keep you all posted.
Love from Hospital World,
Christo

June 21, 7:30 am
From the WFB Medical Desk, this just in. . . .

Today's med bulletin: heart rate 120. He's atrial-fibrillating. Heart rate was 40 Monday. Normal is 60. They're treating it.

His creatonin level (sp?—a kidney chemical thing) is 5.8. Normal is 1.5. At 6, they start considering dialysis.

At this point he has less than 10% of his kidney function. But there are a few small encouraging signs that his kidneys are starting slowly to regenerate, having to do with details that I think I'll spare you.

He's very, very weak, not terribly coherent. Every other time he speaks it's to say, "I have to get my train ticket." I'm trying to figure out where it is he wants to go. (Don't ask.)

Will keep you posted.
Much love,

Friday, June 22, 2007
9 am
WFB Medical Bulletin

So his kidneys are *trying* to regenerate. There are good indications and some less good. For those of you who hang on my creatinine level reports (I must really learn how to spell it), it's now 6.3. You'll remember from my much-praised Bulletin #1 that normal is 1.5. The attentive among you will remember from yesterday's bulletin that it was 5.8. The good part is that the rate of increase has slowed. You will be responsible for this on the final exam. The urine report I will keep to myself, if you don't mind, but I will say this much: he is a river to his people.

In other WFB Organ News, he's still "fibbing." Nothing to do with mendacity, but rather the term us medical-types use for "fibrillating."

His heart rate is in the 100 range. Normal is about 60. Monday his was 40—definitely not good, so you can see he is making excellent progress there.

No appetite, I regret to say, but I am feeding him little delicious bits of Julian's snacks.*

Mental alertness–wise we are sort of in and out. He's not conversational, though he can be toward the end of the day when the meds lie quieter in his blood. At which point he reverts to his default imperious position. Last night at 7 he instructed me that he wanted a Macintosh laptop computer, "Right now," so that he could write a column "at two am, in case I wake up." He was not im-

---

*His beloved peanut-butter-and-bacon sandwiches. They became very popular with the nursing staff.

pressed by my pleas that I would not be able, at this late hour of the day, to a) supply him with a wireless-enabled computer and an operating system alien to him, and to b) train him on said computer in "less than an hour," to quote his demand verbatim. Doubtless this evening he will stir and castigate me for my delinquency, to say nothing of my obtuseness. But then I have never masqueraded as a perfect son.

Dialysis-wise, we're at the let's-give-it-another-day stage. I can't emphasize what superb care he is getting at the Stamford Hospital. Was I surprised to learn that Dr. Hines, his kidney doctor, turns out to be a Yale man? Not one bit. I had been a bit worried that he was Harvard, but am now at peace on that score.

He is doing his best and sends you his best love, as do I.

WFB Medical Bulletin
June 23

Arrived at the hospital at 7 this morning, bearing 50 "munchkin" donuts from Dunkin' Donuts with which to jolly the (truly lovely) nursing staff.

WFB greeted me stony-faced and furious: *"WHY HAVEN'T THEY OF-FERED US A **COCKTAIL**?"*

I had no good answer to this. He thereupon said, leaving no doubt as to the urgency, "I need a Stilnox. *Now.*" (Stilnox, those of you familiar with the WFB Pharmacological Encyclopedia—Vol. XXVI—will recognize as his "definitive" Swiss sleeping pills.) While I stammered fecklessly that perhaps we might wait until the doctors had made their rounds before we rendered him comatose, he fell immediately asleep.

Urine-wise, until now I have endeavored to spare you details about this aspect. But the high volume of reader mail suggests that you will not be denied every detail. Have it your way.

Until now, I had never imagined that my happiness could be contingent on the color of my father's urine. (My life used to be more exciting, really.)

Today's is . . . how do I describe today's? I would describe it as the color of a fine Riesling: umber, full-bodied, with hints of creatinine and red blood cells with a nice finish. This is a vast improvement over the Coca-Cola hue of 48 hours ago. Volume-wise, I repeat yesterday's med bulletin: He is a river to his people.

He wants to go home. Every other sentence he utters is about that. I want that too for him. Very much. But we're not there yet. My mantra, with which he is out of patience—and I don't blame him—is: "Let's just take it day by day. And see."

He sends his best love, as do I.

WFB Medical Bulletin
Sunday, June 24

The daily creatinine report: 6.4. Those of you who made it through yesterday's WFB Medical Bulletin will recall that it was at 6.5. So this is simply splendid news.

But wait, there's more. Since yesterday afternoon, he has been "back on sinus rhythm." It means, to put it in terms you simple (and, I am sure, decent and good) folk can understand: we are no longer "fibbing." (As in "defibrillating.")

Are we out of the woods? No. Are we going home today? No—a point I spend perhaps 90% of my conversational time with him having to reiterate. (It's like being on *Firing Line*, on acid.)

"Have you packed my things?"

"Em, well, uh, no, Pup, not precisely. I . . ."

"Why?"

"Well, em, there's the matter of, em, the fact that your kidneys aren't functioning, plus you can't breathe or move. Apart from that—"

"I can breathe at **home**."

"Yes. Yes, certainly. You've—ha—got me there. Ha ha. Yup. Will you have another sip of the milkshake for me? They say it's got all the essential—"

"What time is our reservation on the train?"

"The train. Yes. I'm working on that. But it seems the, um, bridge is washed out north of Bridgeport, so, you know, a few . . . problems."

"We'll need music."

"Absolutely."

Tomorrow his regular doctors will return from their weekend frolics—no weekend frolics for this correspondent, whose motto continues to be "Tomorrow Is Another Day."

He sends his best love, as do I.

WFB Medical Bulletin
June 26

Today's new term is "effective urine."

What—pray—is "effective urine"? I myself did not, until several hours ago, know this phrase. Essentially, it is that which carries with it out of the body things like creatinine—a chemical the very name of which I am beginning heartily to loathe. What we seek, what we pray for, what we want even more than our own front teeth this Christmas this year is—effective urine. Is this really too much to ask for?

In other news:

We have a drip in our arm to keep us hydrated.

Spirits: let's face it, ten days in hospital, however nice the hospital, and this place is very good indeed, are not fun, especially if you are the author of books like *Cruising Speed* and *Airborne*.[*]

He wants to go home.

He wants to have dinner tonight at Paone's.

He wants me to call his barber to make an appointment.

He wants to write his column.

He wants to work on his (excellent) Goldwater book.

---

[*]WFB books (1971 and 1984), each about a single week in his life, in which he seemed to pack more than most people do in a lifetime. David Brooks's savage parody of the latter book, in a University of Chicago student publication, led Pup to offer him his first job; the rest is history.

He wants to go sailing with Van and Alistair.

He wants me to get him his Ritalin. He decided yesterday to start calling it "Rossignol," making for an interesting conversation.

He wants not to hear me say, "Now, Pup, I think maybe we ought to leave the catheter in just one more day." (Let me point out that I do not say this to him, 20 times a day, because I have nothing else to do.)

He wants a chocolate milkshake. (Which I have been smuggling in to him. I did this after taking one small taste of the "hi-protein" milkshake provided by the hospital.)

He does not want visitors, but he loves you all very much.

He wants to be well.

He wants not to hear the words "urine" or "creatinine" or "blood work." Doubtless, he would prefer not to hear the word "kidneys," though we—that is, I—are very much wanting these organs to get with the program and heal themselves.

At any rate, we (Stockholm syndrome first person plural) are neither better nor worse. But we remain confident that the kidneys will, recognizing their role in amongst the other organs of a great and beloved man, soon get with the program and repair themselves *tout court*.

Meantime we send you all our best love. I fully expect tomorrow's WFB Medical Bulletin to begin with "Hosanna!"

**WFB Medical Bulletin
July 1, 2007 (Mum's birthday)**

Pup came home on Friday. He is, I can say as his spokesperson, "resting comfortably."

Urine Report: There will be no

further urine reports. I know this will come as a terrible shock to many of you. Sorry, but you're on your own. If you want a urine report, just look down next time you go to the loo.

CHAPTER 9

I Miss My Urine Report

He arrived home by ambulance, and was carried upstairs to his room by two beefy young men. On their way out, one of them said to me in a lowered voice, "He's DNR, right?" I started a bit but, recovering, said, "Yeah." DNR means Do Not Resuscitate. If those are your wishes, you apply to your doctor and are given a letter from the state of

Connecticut, signed by the doctor, instructing emergency medical technicians not to bring you back from the brink. Such were indeed Pup's wishes. Along with the form comes a red plastic bracelet. The young man said, "If something happens, make sure he's wearing the bracelet." I nodded and pressed beer money on them.

Pup was home, but he was very, very ill. His bedroom, looking out on Long Island Sound, was now cluttered with noisy machines to help him breathe.

I'd arranged for day and night nurses. I specified that they must be . . . well, Pup was not one to suffer chatterboxes. One of Mum's nurses had been on the talkative side. She was an Italian-Polish lady (her surname, with lots of z's and k's and g's, would have won a Scrabble tournament). She was built like a bomb shelter and had interesting flame red and purple hair. She would talk indefatigably throughout her six-hour, $465 shifts. If she left the room, Mum would groan, "She is *driving me to drink*." But she was a good lady with a warm heart, and in the final battle with Mum, she didn't yield an inch. And believe me, the wrath of Pat Buckley could instill fear in an advancing column of mechanized infantry.

In the hospital two days before she died, Mum had demanded that she give her her own sleeping pills. As you can see, self-medication was a theme with my parents.

"No, ma'am," she replied coolly. "We're in the hospital. In the *critical care* unit."

"I am well aware of where I am. Just give. Me. My. Pills."

"No, ma'am. I can't give you pills."

"Just. *Give. Them. To. Me.*"

"No, ma'am."

At this, Mum's lower mandible protruded like that thing in the movie *Alien*, just before swallowing an astronaut whole. "Just . . . *give* . . . *them. . . to me.*"

"No, ma'am. I will give them to your hospital nurse here, and *she* can give them to you if the doctor says it's all right."

This was the last conversation I heard my mother have.

As for Pup, I felt, pharmacology-wise, that the ideal nurses for him would be, say, sight-impaired deaf-mutes. Pup's daily intake of pills would be enough to give Hunter Thompson pause. But there was hardly any point in turning his sickroom into a home rehab.

The third afternoon in the hospital, after Pup had rallied somewhat, he demanded that I give him an after-lunch Ritalin from his private stash. Inasmuch as I had spent the previous three nights wide awake and physically restraining him from ripping tubes out of his arms and trying to flee the hospital, I was of the opinion that Ritalin might not—as we medical types put it—be indicated, and I refused to give him one.

"Just give it to me," he growled.

"I am not going to give you a Ritalin. For heaven's sake, Pup—you're fibrillating."

"Just give it to me."

"No." Moment of truth.

"You're fired," he said.

"Fine!" I said. "I didn't ask for this job in the first place."

We agreed on a compromise. If Gavin said he could have one, fine, party down. He phoned Gavin, who I imagine rolled his eyes and okayed a minimal Ritalin. I spent the afternoon catering to the myriad whims of my suddenly very peppy father.

Desperate times call for desperate measures. I entered into a conspiracy with the nurses. We worked out a Kabuki dance whereby Pup would ask for his Ritalin, and they'd give him a similar-looking Ativan pill, placing it directly on his tongue before he could inspect it.

"I don't understand why I'm *sleeping* so much," he would say to me, rousing hours later from a narcoleptic slumber.

"Well, Pup," I said, avoiding eye contact, "you know, these kidney things, they, uh, do take it out of you."

Henry Kissinger called. "I miss your urine reports," he said in his rumbly Teutonic baritone. I told him this was surely the first time he had uttered those words.

Pup and Henry went back a long way: to the mid-1950s, when Henry was a young history professor at Harvard. He'd asked Pup, then the fresh prince of belles-lettres conservatism, to come speak to his students. A friendship formed and, over the years, deepened. In 1968, with Vietnam raging and a bitter presidential campaign going on, Henry, now an adviser to Nelson Rockefeller, had called Pup and said to him, *Get this message through to Nixon: If Vietnam falls, word will go out that while it may be dangerous to be America's enemy, it is fatal to be her friend.* Pup called it in to John Mitchell. After the election, Mitchell summoned Henry to Nixon's transition headquarters at the Pierre Hotel in Manhattan. The rest, you know.

Pup was no fan of détente with the Soviet Union and China, which in the Buckley household was always referred to as "Red China." After Nixon's China opening in 1972, Pup commented wryly in a *Playboy* article that upon receiving the news of Henry's secret visit to Mao, "I broke wind, with heavy philosophical reservation." But through it all, Pup's devotion to and respect for Henry never flickered, and he defended him fiercely against those on the Right who wanted Henry Kissinger's Commie-coddling head on a pike. One of Pup's formulations, which I thought artful, was: *How can Henry Kissinger be, simultaneously, their* [the

Left's] *enemy and* our *enemy?* That usually shut them up, though not for long.

There were one or two moments when Pup did come close to exasperation, as he did the day the news broke that Henry's new boss, President Gerald Ford, had declined to meet with Aleksandr Solzhenitsyn. To Pup, Solzhenitsyn was a secular saint. He stood in awe of him—and there were not that many men who inspired such awe in my old man. That the president of the United States had been too busy—the laughably pathetic excuse offered by the White House spokesperson—to meet with someone Pup called "the voice of baptized humanity" was, well, just a bit . . . too . . . much.*

---

*From Secretary of State Kissinger's memo to President Ford: "Solzhenitsyn is a notable writer, but his political views are an embarrassment even to his fellow dissidents. . . . Not only would a meeting with the president offend the Soviets, but it would raise some controversy about Solzhenitsyn's view of the United States and its allies."

I pestered Pup to find out from—as I put it with callow truculence—"your pal Henry Kissinger" why President Ford was cold-shouldering the author of *The Gulag Archipelago*. Pup sighed at the lunch table. He eventually reported that he had had a little come-to-Jesus with his pal Henry and that Henry had sounded a bit sheepish about it all. As memory serves, he told Pup, *What can I tell you, Bill? It was a busy day, the call came in, I had five seconds to make the decision. It was a mistake and I regret it.* Pup shrugged. He had a mantra that he trotted out when confronted with a situation not to his liking but beyond his control: "And there it is."* There were

---

*In the play and movie *Amadeus,* the Austro-Hungarian emperor says something similar when he's confronted with an unpleasant fact: "Well, there it is." He manages it with a wonderful, self-exculpatory shrug of the shoulders, intending to convey an ironic yet humble awareness of his powerlessness, despite—of course—being emperor of half of Europe.

other contentions between the two of them over the years, some of them acute, but they loved each other deeply. I promised Henry that if there were any spectacular developments urine-wise, he would be the first to hear.

One night about two-thirty a.m., Margaret, Pup's sweet and pleasingly taciturn night nurse, shook me awake to say that he wanted to see me right away. I staggered down the hall, heavy-lidded. He was lying athwart his bed, which had become an eagle's nest of printed matter—newspapers, magazines, books—CDs, tissue boxes, and sundry detritus. I could hear Mum's ghost: *Bill, look at this bed. It is disgusting.* The lights were blazing, the TV blaring, oxygen machine chugging. His Cavalier King Charles spaniels, Sebbie and Daisy, yapped stridently at my approach. We had known one another, these doggies and I, for—what?—three years, but they still felt the need to treat my arrivals in their master's bedroom as if I were Charles Manson. They are the most beautiful dogs in God's kingdom, Cavaliers, and almost certainly the dumbest.

Pup had on his *bata* (bathrobe). His hair was all over the place. His faux tortoiseshell glasses, perched askew on his nose, gave him a sort of mad-professor look. I relaxed. He didn't seem in extremis.

"Yes, Pup?" I yawned.

"Christo," he said, "I have something *very important* to discuss with you."

Uh-oh, I thought. *You're leaving* all *your money to* National Review?

"All right," I said cautiously, "I'm listening."

"I think we ought to invite to lunch—*tomorrow*—some very important players in the conservative community."

Relieved as I was that my patrimony was not going to *NR*, I was somewhat at a loss. "Well," I said, "gosh. I think that's a really . . . wonderful idea."

I lay down wearily across the foot of his bed, Daisy lapping at my face, Sebbie demanding to have his tummy scratched, their having decided I had come in peace to their master's nocturnal levee.

"But I mean," Pup emphasized, "*only* serious *players.*"

"Absolutely . . ." I yawned. "So, who'd you have in mind?"

"Well," he said, "we *have* to have McFadden."

I nodded. Jim McFadden, *National Review*'s longtime associate publisher, had died in 1998.

"Right," I said. "We can't not have Jim. I'll, uh, see if he's available."

Pop dictated to me his list of invitees. Some of them were alive. After five minutes of dictation, perhaps punchy, I suggested— inasmuch as he had been working on a memoir of his friendship with Barry Goldwater—that we invite Goldwater. Pup appeared to weigh this, then stared at me querulously.

"Christo," he said, sounding faintly annoyed, "Barry Goldwater is *dead*."

"Right," I said, yawning, "good point."

He wasn't ready for visitors, so for company it was just me and Danny. Danny lived in my old apartment above the garage. For twenty years, Mum and Pup had rented it out to tenants, to help pay the taxes. One tenant, in the 1950s, was a man named Charles Blair.

One fine summer day in the early 1970s, we were having lunch on the terrace, Pup, Mum, me, one or two guests. A car pulled up the driveway. "I wonder who that could be?" Mum said. A tall, lean, handsome man approached. My parents peered, then exclaimed almost in unison, "Charley! For heaven's sake!"

It was Charley Blair, their old tenant. He was in the neighborhood and thought to stop by. What makes this otherwise quite dull story of interest is that Charley, while living over our garage, had been a top pilot for Pan American. On the side, he was working for the CIA, training Francis Gary Powers how to fly the U-2 spy plane. (Powers was shot down by Soviet missiles, resulting in one of the more embarrassing episodes of the cold war.) Charley, meanwhile, continuing to cut a dashing figure, had gone on to marry the actress Maureen O'Hara (my personal platonic ideal of womanhood). After that, he started an air-boat service in the U.S. Virgin Islands. Not quite end of story. Meanwhile:

Charley sat and reminisced with us over iced teas for, I suppose, forty-five minutes or so, at which point Pup said, "How's Maureen?"

"Oh, fine," Charley said. "She's in the car."

"In—the car?" my mother said, appalled. "Do you mean to say, all this time you left her in the *car*?" It was a warm summer day.

"Yeah." Charley shrugged. "She'll be fine, really."

Mum and Pup protested vehemently that he must ask her to come in. Charley shrugged reluctantly, as if asking one of the world's most famous actresses—his wife, incidentally—to join us at the table would be an intolerable imposition. My parents would have none of it, and at length Charley was prevailed upon to fetch his suffocating wife. He returned with the radiant, if slightly wilted, Maureen O'Hara. Eudosia, our ancient beloved, toothless Cuban cook, word having reached her in the kitchen of the arrival on *la terraza* of *la grande estrella Señora O'Hara*, rushed in her slippers to the window that looked out onto the terrace and remained there, watching intently for the duration of the visit.

I gathered, from things I read here and there in later years, that the two of them were inseparable, to the point where Ms. O'Hara got a pilot's license so that she could accompany Charley as co-pilot on his flights. One day, picking up my *New York Times*, I saw on the front page that Charley, unaccompanied by his wife, had been killed in the crash of one of his boat planes.

CHAPTER 10

You Can Imagine How Pleased Your Mother Was

We settled into a routine of sorts, which somewhat depended on how many sleeping pills Pup had self-administered during the night.

I did not, as a young *bacchante* in the sixties and seventies, absent myself from the garden of herbal and pharmacological delights—far from it—so I found myself in an ironic position, lecturing a parent about drugs. The child/parent relationship inevitably reverses, but to this degree I had not anticipated.

Pup, I would say, eyeing the half-empty blister pack of Stilnox by his bedside, *how many Stilnoxes did we take last night?*

I don't know. One and a half? Two?

Two? [Examing the pack, which looked as if it had been half eaten by wolverines in the night.] Two. Okay.

I may have taken another.

Another. So—three, say?

[Becoming annoyed.] There might have been one more.

How many Rits* did we take yesterday?

[Fully annoyed.] What does Rit have to do with not sleeping?

I still can't say, a year later, whether this stunner of a rhetorical statement was simply denial or a *Firing Line*-quality countergambit. I'd made the (really pretty obvious) point to Pup, perhaps, oh, fifty times over recent years, that Ritalin, which he took as a stimulant, was not a means toward a good night's sleep—especially if you took your final one of the day at dinnertime and washed it down with coffee. (While living in Mexico in the early 1950s, my parents

---

*Our nickname for Ritalin. Giving a drug a cute diminutive name somehow domesticates it, though I don't know if that would be possible with, say, methamphetamine. Methy-weth? Driving down a road in rural Maine, my son, Conor, remarked to me that the neighborhood had become "kind of meth-labby."

acquired a taste for coffee so strong, it could revive a three-thousand-year-dead Egyptian mummy and make it run the Boston Marathon; and win.) Oddly, Pup found it difficult to get to sleep after these postprandial attachings of jumper cables to his cortex, and sought to counteract them with "one or two" Stilnoxes. These would knock him out for an hour or so, at which point he would awaken, and, semistuporous, gnaw open the blister pack and swallow God only knows how many more. It did not make for the kind of night's rest you see in the TV ads, with butterflies fluttering above the pillows; more like *Night of the Living Dead.*

It occurs to me that in this increasing dependence, Pup had come to resemble another great Catholic author: Evelyn Waugh. I don't mean to adduce a tropism to sleeping pills among aging Catholic apologists, but—there it is. Waugh's addiction to paraldehyde, a popular "sleeping draught" of the 1950s, combined with his alcoholism, drove him to the breakdown he limned fictionally in his late-career novel *The Ordeal of Gilbert Pinfold*, a story of one very hairy ride through the subconscious. In any event, Pup's reliance on uppers and downers was not hastening his recovery. But short of tying him down and confiscating his meds, there wasn't a whole heck of a lot I could do about it. His youngest sister, my aunt Carol, was adamant that he be "detoxed," to which I responded, "Be my guest."

Pup's self-medicating was, I venture, a chemical extension of the control he asserted over every other aspect of his life. The term *control freak* is pejorative. I'd put it this way: Few great men—and I use the term precisely, for Pup was a great man—do *not* seek to assert total control over their domains. Winston Churchill, to pick one, wasn't the type to shrug, "Oh, well, whatever. Go with the flow." I revere Mark Twain, but I'd say that for all his devotion to his family, he was moderately impossible as a father and husband.* Great men (and yes of course by that I include women) tend to be the stars of their own movies.

Some years ago, I came across a quote that could serve as the solipsist's definitive credo: "Let me have my own way exactly in everything, and a sunnier and pleasanter creature does not exist." (Thomas Carlyle)† Pup never plunged

---

*Twain was in many ways a doting father, but as his avatar Hal Holbrook observes, "I think the fun would have had to go *his* way." Twain's contemporary Herman Melville, on the other hand, did shrug and go with the flow, and what's more, left us Bartleby, the Scrivener ("I would prefer not to"), the most famous recalcitrant in literature.

†How very weird and ironic that the author of this excellent sentiment should have endured one of the worst accidents that could befall an author, as he did when John Stuart Mill's absentminded parlor maid tossed volume 1 of his manuscript of *The French Revolution* into the fireplace after Carlyle dozed off in the parlor, awaiting his friend's return.

into bad moods or became grouchy if things didn't go his way, perhaps for the reason that they always went his way. He was invariably the sunniest and most pleasant creature in the room. The moods of those in attendance upon him—Mum's, mainly—did not always match his in the sunny and pleasant departments. Point is, great men tend to want things to go their way.

A remote control, say, in the hands of an autocrat of the TV room becomes a *Star Trek* phaser gun set on stun. Evenings, if Pup was up to it, Danny and I would bring him down in the electric rail chair and then, slowly—he had to stop every three feet and gasp for air—to the music room. The three of us would eat one of Julian's delicious meals on trays and watch a movie. I say "movie," but "movies" would be more accurate, since five minutes in, he would, without bothering to say, "Let's watch something else," simply change the channel. One day, when I called from away, Danny reported with a somewhat strained chuckle, "We watched parts of five movies last night."

This was not a new habit of his. He and Mum might be watching with half a dozen guests *Murder on the Orient Express* when, just as a key plot point was being introduced, suddenly the screen would fill with a documentary on Che Guevara or the Tuareg nomads of the sub-Sahara. I wonder: Does the FBI keep crime statistics on murder committed by family members of serial channel changers?

All this seems very trivial now, but at the time, Pup's death grip on the remote took on a sort of proxy significance, emblematic as it was of the control he exerted over the solar system he inhabited. Once or twice during the convalescence, I became so splutteringly frustrated, after the fourth or fifth channel change, that I silently stormed out of the room, leaving poor Danny to cope. *He's sick*, I would tell myself, fuming off to my room. But halfway up the stairs, my inner noodge would whisper, *Well, yeah, but it's not quite* that *simple, is it?*

For my parents' fortieth wedding anniversary in 1990, I did a video in the form of a mock episode of *60 Minutes*. I taped interviews with thirty or so of their friends and even persuaded a sporting Mike Wallace to play along with an ambush interview of himself in which he flees the interviewer (me), protesting, "I find these kinds of interviews *distasteful*!"

One of the interviews was of Pup's great friend Dick Clurman ("the perfect Christian") and his wife, Shirley. Dick and Shirley had accompanied my parents on perhaps a dozen Christmas cruises aboard chartered sailboats in the Caribbean. In the interview, Dick, standing in his Manhattan apartment dressed in yellow foul-weather gear, describes how it was one Christmas Eve on one of the cruises.

Everything was perfect. Mum had brought and wrapped presents for everyone, placing them around a Christmas tree she had contrived. (God, she was brilliant at Christmases, Mum.) She'd even brought and strung up little twinkly lights. Drinks were served. "Silent Night" was playing on the CD player. The boat was anchored in the most charming, lovely, beautiful, protected cove in the entire Caribbean. (You see where this is going?) Everything was perfect.

At which point Pup suddenly decided that it would be even more perfect if they up-anchored and moved across the way to a different cove. Mum said, *Bill, just* leave *it*. But leaving it was not Bill's way. No, no. Ho, ho, ho. Dick's recitation of what followed is quite hilarious, but I imagine it was very far from hilarious at the time.

Pup ordered the anchor up, and as they proceeded across the bay, a sudden squall hit, drenching everything, washing presents overboard, shorting out the Christmas lights, knocking over the tree; whereupon, in the dark and confusion, the yacht went aground. So instead of spending a lovely, calm Christmas Eve in the protected cove, listening to "White Christmas" with the twinkly lights, they spent it in the dark, at a forty-five-degree angle atop a sandbar, in a rainstorm. All because Pup had insisted that it would be "*much* nicer over on the other side." Great men are not content to leave well enough alone.

"So that was Christmas Eve," Dick concludes in the interview. Shirley, next to him, is at this point convulsed with laughter. "You can imagine how pleased your mother was," he says.

Yes, I could. I'd been there many times.

CHAPTER 11

My Old Man and the Sea*

❦

Pup was an avid sailor. He had learned to sail as a child in upstate Connecti-

---

*Title gleefully stolen from the wonderful book by Daniel and David Hays, the first father-son team to sail around Cape Horn. (What *were* they thinking?) Pup reviewed the book for *The New York Times,* and it became a big best seller.

cut, on a not very large lake. Now we lived on the Connecticut shore of Long Island Sound and kept a thirty-eight-foot wooden sloop. It was named *Panic*, a name my mother found all too apt.

In his garage office study, there is a framed photograph of *Panic*. It was taken by a news photographer at the start of the 1958 Newport–Bermuda race. In it, *Panic* is lying on its side at a more or less ninety-degree angle, its mast submerged in the water. This undesirable nautical posture is called a "knock-down." It was thrilling for me as a six-year-old to hear my father's crewmates describe the sensation of thousands of gallons of the Atlantic pouring into the cabin at the start of a five-day ocean race.

I now "get" that Pup's greatness was of a piece with the way he conducted himself at sea. Great men always have too much canvas up. Great men take great risks. It's the timorous souls—

souls like myself—who err on the side of caution; who take in sail when they see a storm approaching and look for snug harbor. Not my old man. Or as Mum used to put it, "Bill, why are you trying to kill us?"

Great men are also impatient. This particular aspect showed up most vividly in my father's manner of docking his boats.

Most people, when guiding, say, a ten- or twenty-ton vessel toward a dock, approach slowly. Not my old man. His technique was to go straight at it, full speed. Why waste time? This made for memorable episodes.

At one point in his life, he owned a seventy-two-foot-long schooner. It had an eighteen-foot-long bowsprit. With my father at the wheel, going hell-bent for leather toward a pier, that long bowsprit became a jousting lance. What vivid memories I have of people scattering like sheep at our approach. One time, someone actually leapt off the dock into the water in an attempt to escape. Over the years, my father took out entire sections of docks up and down the eastern seaboard. His crew bestowed on him the nickname "Captain Crunch."

When I was six, he contrived a treasure hunt. He bought an antique wooden chest and filled it with silver dollars. Also with some of my mother's jewelry. He and a friend sailed across Long Island Sound one weekend and buried it on a sandy spit called on the chart Eaton's Neck but which I will always call "Treasure Island."

He told me that he had come into possession of an old treasure map. It was something out of Robert Louis Stevenson, scratched on thick parchment in bloodred ink. The location of the treasure was indicated with compass bearings. I couldn't sleep the night before we set out, I was so excited.

We sailed across. After digging up half of Eaton's Neck, we found the treasure. I can still remember the thrill as my fingers scraped the chest's wooden lid beneath the sand. When we got home, my father said it would be a nice gesture to give my mother the pirate jewelry. Okay, I said grudgingly, but I was keeping the silver dollars.

It had been such an adventure that I persuaded my father there must be another chest buried there somewhere. I was quite persistent. In due course, he relented and procured another chest, which he filled with another fistful of my mother's jewels, this time adding— without telling her—a few pieces of her prized Queen Anne silver. He sailed across and buried it.

On the weekend appointed for the treasure hunt, Hurricane Donna struck. Donna was a Katrina of her day. She hit with such force that she rearranged the entire topography of Eaton's Neck, making nonsense of the compass bearings on the treasure map.

We sailed over the next weekend. We dug and dug. And dug. By the time we were finished, Eaton's Neck looked as if it had been ravaged by a thousand prairie dogs. We never did find the treasure. For all we know, it's still there.

How thrilled my mother was to learn that her jewels and Queen Anne silver were now a permanent geological feature of Eaton's Neck. I wonder what the reaction of the insurance company was.

I'm not sure I understand. Was the jewelry stolen, Mr. Buckley?

No, we buried it. Is there a problem?

The next hurricane landed poor old *Panic* atop the Stamford Harbor breakwater. My father used that insurance payment to buy a successor yacht, a sweet, forty-two-foot Sparkman & Stephens yawl, Hong Kong built. She was named *Suzy Wong,* and she was a real honey, all teak and mahogany and carved Buddhas.

Every summer, we would cruise the waters of Maine aboard *Suzy*. Sailing in Maine was always an adventure. The water is scrotum-tighteningly cold, the currents swift, the tidal drop pronounced, and the bottom unforgivingly rocky.

We'd drop anchor, a maneuver called "kedging," have a merry, kerosene-lamplit dinner, and then drift off to sleep. Soon, invariably, there'd be a sound under the hull: *thunk, thunk, thunk*. This announced beyond reasonable doubt that our kedge had slipped and that we were now positioned over a sharp rock, on a falling tide. Depending on how many bottles of wine had been consumed, the grown-ups were not always quick to respond. In due course, my mother's voice would call out in the dark, "Bill, what do you propose to do about that *sound*?"

My mother deserves a word of appreciation here. She was a dutiful yachtsman's wife. Lord, how she worked at it. In earlier times, the term for this occupation was "galley slave." She had been raised as a debutante, a beautiful, delicate orchid from Vancouver, Canada. Now she found herself cooking for eight men and scrubbing the toilet aboard a small boat with no hot water. She would mutter darkly, "I was made for better things."

In those nonrefrigerated, premicrowave days, a lot of our food came in tins. These were stored below the floorboards in the ship's bilges. The bilges invariably filled with oily seawater, causing the labels to decompose. As a result, we never knew what, exactly, we'd be having for dinner on any given night. If we were lucky, Dinty Moore beef stew. If not, we might well dine exclusively on Harvard beets and creamed corn. Some tins contained crêpes suzette. My father, no cook himself, loved to douse them in copious amounts of Grand Marnier. At the climactic moment, he would drop a match into the skillet, causing a Hiroshima of flame to lick the cabin top. Again, my mother's voice was heard: "Bill, why are you trying to set fire to the boat?"

Some afternoons, my father might say, "Shall we have lobster tonight?" He'd steer for the nearest lobster pot. As a child, I found this thrilling beyond belief, for it was established lore that a Maine lobsterman could legally shoot you on sight if he caught you plundering his livelihood.

After laborious heavings on the line, the trap would come up, suddenly alive with frantic, jackknifing lobsters. The trick was getting them out without having them clamp down on your fingers. My father would then put two bottles of whiskey into the lobster pot as payment. I always wondered what the lobsterman thought upon bringing up his trap, to find two fifths of Johnnie Walker Black inside. Did he scratch his head and say, "Reckon Mr. Buckley is back"?

Sometimes we barbecued on a little grill that hung off the transom. One night, as I was cooking six expensive filet mignons that Mum had asked me *please* not to burn, the grill suddenly swiveled 180 degrees. Six expensive filet mignons and charcoal briquettes plopped hissingly into the dark, swift waters of Penobscot Bay.

It was either rescue the filet mignons or another night of Harvard beets. My friend Danny and I grabbed a flashlight and leapt into the dinghy. We fired up the outboard and roared off into the night. The current was running five knots. It was tricky work corraling those fugitive filets. We ran a few of them over with the outboard propeller, turning them into Salisbury steaks. No one asked for salt that night.

Such were our adventures. Larger ones loomed.

My father had always had the notion of sailing across the Atlantic, and this we did in 1975. The story is told in his book *Airborne*. We set off from Miami on June 1. A month and forty-four hundred miles later, we dropped anchor in the shadow of Gibraltar.

He taught me on that trip how to navigate by the sun and stars with a sextant. It's a skill that today, in the age of satellite navigation, fewer fathers impart to their sons. As I look back, it seems to me one of the most fundamental skills a father can teach a son: finding out where you are, using the tools of our ancestors.

I was twenty-three now. I'd spent a year between high school and college working on a Norwegian tramp freighter. I'd gone around the world, been in rough situations among rough people. I'd steered a twenty-thousand-ton ship through sixty-foot seas in a force ten gale in the South Atlantic. I knew my way around a boat.

One midnight, I relieved my father on the twelve-to-four watch. He told me to put on my safety harness. "Yeah," I said, "don't worry, I'll get around to it." He let me have it, in harsh words—perhaps the second time in twenty-three years he'd spoken to me that way. Falling overboard at night in the middle of the ocean without a safety harness is not a thing to be taken lightly.

I obeyed, but later that night, still simmering over my affronted manhood, I made an entry in the log to the effect that Captain Crunch could take his safety harness and shove it where the sun don't shine. The next morning, upon examining the log, he smiled, delighted at the mutiny.

What a trip it was! We sailed into the Azores, accompanied by a thousand dolphins; camped out in the crater of an extinct volcano; sailed through the spot where Nelson sank the French and Spanish fleets; and finally reached the place that had once been called the Pillars of Hercules, end of the known world.

We had such a good time, in fact, that Pup declared that we must sail across the Pacific, from Honolulu to New Guinea. We did, ten years later.

I was now thirty-three, recently married.

"By the way," I said to my new bride on our honeymoon, trying to sound casual, "I won't be around much this summer."

Lucy was a pretty good sport about it. The first time I'd brought her to Stamford to meet my parents, my father insisted on taking us out for a cocktail sail. It was a bright, beautiful summer day, but the wind was blowing about twenty-five knots, with six-foot seas.

She had been in a sailboat exactly once before, on a lake, in flat, calm water. The waves crashed over the cockpit, hurling her to the deck. She smiled bravely and said, "Is it *always* like this?"

My mother, hearing this account after we got home, drenched to the skin, remarked acerbically, "Yes, Lucy. With Bill, it is *always* like that."

Off we set across the great Pacific.

We made our first landfall a week later, at a strange little archipelago called Johnston Atoll. It's here that the United States stores its most lethal nerve-gas weapons and God knows what else. For that reason, any ship sailing into the harbor is greeted not by lovely island girls bearing leis and rum punches, but by grim-faced Halliburton contractors aiming .50-caliber machine guns at you. Welcome to Johnston Atoll!

We made our peaceful intentions clear to the frowning colonel in charge. It was an ironic encounter, for that same day, back home in Stamford, Nancy Reagan, then first lady of the United States, was spending the weekend at our house with my mother. The colonel was unimpressed with my father's desperate name-dropping and informed us dourly that we must be on our way.

Somewhere between Johnston Atoll and our next port of call, we caught a dolphin (the mahi-mahi type, not the Flipper type). We were thrilled at our good fortune, as by now we were down to the detested Harvard beets and squishy, malodorous rotting fruit.

We hauled the fish aboard—a beautiful, iridescent creature. I reluctantly prepared to deal the coup de grâce with a heavy winch handle. No, no, someone said: Pour vodka into the gills. It deoxygenates them, producing swift, painless death. I did. It shuddered violently for a second or two and then was still. I recommend this protocol. And if you don't die at first, keep trying. It's a nice way to go.

We made three landfalls on our way

to New Guinea, each one something out of Gauguin. After the weeks at sea, we were avid for R&R; for a swim that didn't involve someone having to stand shark guard with an assault rifle. For cold beer and hot showers. For a stretch of sleep longer than four hours.

But the moment we dropped anchor, my father would look at his watch and say, "Okay, it's ten o'clock now. What say we shove off at two?"

Danny and I would look at each other and shake our heads. I was learning that for my father, it's the voyage, not the stopping. Great men are not dawdlers; their idle is set too high. They're built for speed. I myself was built to lie on the sand and drink beer and be fanned by island girls.

And so at two o'clock, it was up anchor and off to the next idyllic atoll, some thousand miles away. I scribbled in my journal, "We are racing through Paradise." Pup liked that and used it for the title of the book he wrote about the trip.

We did, however, manage to convince him to stop for a whole day at a place called Kapingamarangi. You may not be familiar with Kapingamarangi, but it's there—on the chart, 350 miles northeast of New Guinea. We sailed over the reef into a turquoise lagoon fringed with white sand and swaying coconut palms. Natives came out in a launch to greet us. This was 1985.

"Is there anything you need?" we asked, thinking perhaps batteries, antibiotics, tools.

"Among my people," the headman said gravely, "there is a great hunger for videocassettes."

There was a plane in the lagoon. It was still shiny bright beneath the water. It had been there for forty years. I scuba dived on it; saw the "U.S. Navy" markings and the bullet holes that had brought it down, hem-stitched along the fuselage. A quarter mile away was a sunken Japanese vessel, the object, perhaps, of the American plane's last attack.

"What happened here?" I asked the headman.

He shrugged. "First the Japanese bombed the shit out of it, then the Americans came and bombed the shit out of it." There you have it: World War II in a nutshell.

We were navigating again by sextant and the stars. But Pup had always been on the cutting edge of the latest gadgetry, so we had with us a prototype of a satellite navigation device made by the Trimble company. My father had gone to enormous pains to procure it from his new best friend, Charlie Trimble. It was the size of a steamer trunk and had more dials and knobs and oscilloscopes than Dr. Frankenstein's laboratory. Pup would crouch before it for *endless* hours, twiddling the knobs and calling out numbers to us, which we'd plot on the chart.

"Where does *that* put us?" he would groan hopefully.

"Here," I said, pointing to a spot in the middle of the Brazilian rain forest.

It was back to basics, to the sextant and the stars. He preferred those, anyway. I can still see him standing on the deck at twilight, searching the sky for Spica and Vega and Deneb, one hand wrapped around a stay for support, the sextant in his other, calling out, "Mark!"

A month after sailing out of Honolulu, we anchored in Kavieng Harbor on New Ireland island. That night we had a celebration as liquid as the vast Pacific. I toasted him, "To Pup, who shot the sun, shot the stars, but who most of all shot the moon."

IT WAS OUR LAST LONG SAIL TOGETHER. He was getting older now. So was I. I was a father of two. Then came the episode of October 1997.

We'd made a date the month previous to have an overnight sail to Treasure Island along with Danny, our old sailing partner. I took the train up from Washington, D.C., to Stamford. Along the way, I looked out the window and saw gray, stormy skies. I checked the weather in the paper, where I saw the word *northeaster*. To anyone who's grown up along the Connecticut seashore, this is not a word congruent with "overnight sail."

My father was standing there on the train platform to greet me. This had always been a welcoming sight. But I noticed, through the train window, that he seemed to be holding on to a sign, as if for support. Had he injured himself?

No, for when the train door opened and I went to disembark, a violent gust of northeast wind blew me back into the train. I crawled out, practically on all fours. Loose objects in the railroad parking lot were being blown about. It looked like the tornado scene in *The Wizard of Oz.*

"We'll have a brisk sail," my father said.

Danny was there with him. I looked at Danny. Danny looked at me.

"We're going *out* in this?" I said incredulously.

"Sure," my father said nonchalantly.

We arrived at the marina. The wind gauge indicated steady at forty-five knots, gusting fifty. To put that in context, hurricane-force winds start at sixty-four.

"Pup," I said, shouting to make myself heard above the wind, "*ought* we to be doing this?"

"Take in the fenders," he replied merrily.

He had brought with him a friend of

his from San Francisco. Poor, innocent lamb. He had never been on a sailboat before.

"Should I take a Dramamine?" he asked me nervously.

"Nah," I said. "You'll be too scared to throw up."

And so off we sailed into the storm. This was in my father's last sailboat, a thirty-six-foot fiberglass sloop named *Patito*. (Roughly translated as "Ducky," which my father and mother called each other.)

We somehow made it across Long Island Sound, through a screaming, dark night and fifteen-foot seas. I kept the radio tuned to the Coast Guard frequency. I thought of my two young children. I thought of my warm bed in Washington. I thought, *What the f—— am I doing out here?*

The next morning, after a sleepless night at anchor listening to the halyards slap furiously against the mast, a greasy dawn arrived. The wind had increased; it was now gusting to fifty-five knots. The radio reported that over half a million homes in New England were without power. Various governors had declared a state of emergency. We had gone for an overnight sail in a state of emergency.

I proposed that we row ashore and flag down a passing car, or perhaps a FEMA vehicle.

"No, no," said my father. "We'll be fine."

It was daylight now, so we could see the seas we were up against, and there was nothing pleasant about them. Perhaps you've seen the movie *The Perfect Storm*? Something like that.

We made it—somehow—back across Long Island Sound. My mother had spent the morning on the phone to the Coast Guard. The Coast Guard kept saying, "But Mrs. Buckley, what are they *doing* out there in this?"

Good question, I thought, draining a glass of brandy with trembling hands.

I simmered for a few days and then wrote my father a blistering letter. *Never again*, I vowed.

SINCE THEN, I've taught my own son to sail. I remember the first time I placed his small hands, along with mine, on the tiller and taught him the feel of the boat and the wind and the sea. I thought back to when my father had first taken my small hands in his and taught me the rudiments of the same art. Now I was imparting to my son what my father had passed along to me: something elemental, thrilling, and joyous.

Pup had furled his sails now and was preparing to shove off on a different kind of voyage. I wonder—will the angels scatter as he approaches the Pearly Pier?

I think back to that night in 1997, to

my vow that I would never again set foot on a boat with him. And now I think I'd give almost anything for just one more sail together, even in a howling northeaster.

"A gone shipmate, like any other man," Joseph Conrad wrote, "is gone forever, and I never met one of them again. But at times the spring-flood of memory sets with force up the dark River of the Nine Bends. Then on the waters of the forlorn stream drifts a ship—manned by a crew of Shades. They pass and make a sign, in a shadowy hail. Haven't we, together and upon the immortal sea, wrung out a meaning from our sinful lives? Goodbye, brothers! You were a good crowd. As good a crowd as ever fisted with wild cries the beating canvas of a heavy foresail; or tossing aloft, invisible in the night, gave back yell for yell to a westerly gale."

CHAPTER 12

If It Weren't for
the Religious Aspect

G etting from the house to his garage study, a distance of about fifty
yards, had become difficult for Pup in
the months following Mum's death.
Despite my insistence to the staff and
Danny that he must not be allowed to
get behind the wheel of a vehicle, he

had—prior to the hospitalization—gotten into his red Pontiac Montana minivan one day and driven himself to his study. Later, returning to the house, he had decided it was too irksome to execute a three-point turn and so had backed the van to the house, slamming into an ancient apple tree, resulting in $3,000 damage. He emerged unscathed, luckily, inasmuch as he disdained seat belts, even on long drives. *Please, Pup,* I would plead. *Among other things, it's the law. I'll get a ticket if we're stopped.* His answer, delivered with a dismissive snort: *We won't get stopped.*

Pup's aloofness in the matter of seat belts and stop signs and speed limits and other nuisances had long puzzled me, in a bemused sort of way. As his driving came more to resemble Mr. Toad's Wild Ride at Disneyland, my bemusement diminished. One day Aunt Carol—Pup's youngest sister—and I were chatting. Being the tenth and last of my grandparents' children, Carol has a wry and perceptive take on her siblings. *Oh,* she said with her beguiling and beautiful double-dimpled smile, *don't you understand? The rules don't* apply *to him.* I chuckled and filed it away under "Pup, Mysteries of." When he published his umpteenth book, *Miles Gone By,* a collection of autobiographical pieces, I came across something he had written that unlocked it for me, while in the process making me marvel that he had survived as long as he had.

It was an article he'd written about owning an airplane when he was at Yale. It was called an Ercoupe. He and five other classmates had bought it jointly. One day, one of Pup's friends, a pilot veteran of World War II, bemoaned to him that he badly wanted to see his girlfriend in Boston but had no way of getting there. Pup, ever the gallant, said, "Never fear, I shall *fly* you to Boston!" He had at this point in his flying career exactly one and a half hours of cockpit time. He had never soloed. So he and his friend flew to Boston, the friend doing the flying, which left Pup at Boston Airport all alone and now having to get the plane back to New Haven. I was a licensed pilot in my youth, and I simply shudder to relate the rest of this story.

Pup revs up the Ercoupe for the return flight and takes off, at which point he notices that, gee, it's getting kind of dark. He's neglected to factor in last night's switch from daylight savings to eastern standard time. This being way before GPS, he navigates back toward New Haven in the gloaming by descending to one hundred feet and following *the train tracks*. This somewhat basic mode of navigation begins to fail him when it turns pitch black. The situation now seriously deteriorating, he makes out—thank God—the beacon of the New London airport. He manages to set the plane down there. He then hitchhikes back to New Haven and goes straight to the Fence Club bar to steady his nerves and share his exploits. Next day, his flight instructor, upon learning of the episode, goes completely ballistic.

I'd been unaware of this tale of—what should one call it?—derring-do until I read his piece. (I'm not sure "bravery" is quite the right word, though Pup was the bravest man I knew.) The only Ercoupe anecdote I knew was the one where, flying into Ethel Walker School for his sister Maureen's graduation, he crashed the plane in front of the entire assembly and was carried off the field by the graduating class. As to the moral: A man who would think nothing of flying a plane solo from Boston to New Haven, having had a total of one and a half hours of—well, put it this way, this is not a man who is going to waste a lot of time in life on seat belts, stop signs, or worrying about going for a cocktail cruise in a northeast gale. At any rate, his rear-on collision with the ancient apple tree turned out to be impactful—as it were—not only on the Montana, but on him. After that, he consented to be chauffeured the fifty yards to and from his garage study.

One day, two weeks after his return from the hospital, still ailing badly but bored witless by inertia, he determined to make it to the study and recommence work on his Goldwater memoir. This was valiant. Here he could barely breathe, could barely stand up, could—barely—speak. (The self-administrations of Stilnox didn't help here, but never mind.) Into the bargain, it was blowing a summer gale. We were both drenched to the skin by the time I got him situated in the cockpit of his study. I approached him with the nose oxygen tube. He made a face. We had had, oh, fifty discussions about this.

Let's put in your oxygen tube, okay?

What good would that do?

Well, it's oxygen, you know, and since you're having a hard time breathing—

I don't see what good it does.

[Looping the tubes around his ears and inserting the end into his nostrils.] Well, can't be doing any harm, shouldn't think. . . .

He fired up his computers. He hunched unsteadily over his keyboard. I hovered behind, ready to catch him if he pitched forward.

I'm going to have to dictate to you.

I'm a little rusty at WordStar, Pup. It's been a quarter century.

So he stood, holding on to the edge of his desk for support, and began to dictate the last chapter of his memoir about Barry Goldwater.

The years ahead were, by the standards of Barry Goldwater, unhurried. . . .

I struggled to keep up. I'm a fairly fast touch typist, but WordStar, with its jillion complex key commands, made me feel as if I were at the controls of a steam locomotive.

What amazed me, and still does now, a year later, on reading the final pages in the published Goldwater book, was how fluent it was. I have beside me the just-published book, and rereading the final chapter, I find it remarkably little changed from what issued from Pup's oxygen-deprived blue lips that rainy morning in July in his study. It was as if his mind were a still brightly burning fire deep within the wreckage of his body. He made hardly any self-corrections as he spoke. The words came out punctuated and paragraphed. And quickly. My fingers scuttled across the keyboard like crabs. In less than ten minutes, we were on the last paragraph of the last book he would write.

And that was that. No one else comes to mind who sustained for so long a comparable reputation for candor and courage. Over the years, if active in the political community, one comes across rejected aspirants for the presidency. But even in that rare company Goldwater, whether initiating a call from the South Pole to my wife, or puddle-jumping the Grand Canyon for his friends, was unique, and will forever remain so.

My eyes misted up, typing that. I said, "It's beautiful, Pup."

I searched the menu for the document save. I somehow located the right sequence of keys and pressed them, then held my breath until I saw the chapter file name appear on the screen.

"Let's print it," Pup said.

Here I was stymied.

"I'll do it." He sat down at the keyboard and hit a few keys.

"Oh, *shee-it*." Pup had a way of intensifying the s-word, like one of his complex jazz piano chords. Shit-major-augmented-seventh.

"It's not here," he said.

My heart sank.

"It *was* there," I said.

"Well, it's not here now."

We searched. He phoned Jaime. They spoke in Spanish. Their conversation ended with Jaime saying, *"Lo siento, compadre."* (I'm sorry, my friend.) This did not bode well.

"We'll have to start over," Pup said, sighing.

After some brisk recrimination, a deal was struck. I would retake dictation on the lost coda on the condition that it be on my Mac laptop. I went to fetch it, grumblingly, in the wet.

Pup redictated the chapter, practically verbatim. When we went over it the next day, there was little it needed other than a comma here and a word there.* I was, for the thousandth time in my life, in awe of him.

I remember, as a child, watching him in the car, with his portable blue Olivetti Lettera 32 propped on his knees, pounding out a deadline column. Between 1962 and 2008, he wrote some 5,600 of

---

*The book ends with an anecdote in which I, age twelve at the time, figure. Pup had gotten the details a bit wrong, and I had e-mailed him from Zermatt the correct version. He declined it, saying, "I like my version better." I thought to say, "Pup, it's not a question of liking your version better, but of using the accurate version," but then thought, *Never mind.*

these. Assembled into book form, they would fill forty-five volumes. Add that to his fifty[*] published books and you have ninety-five. This is, I reflect as a fifty-five-year-old author of only thirteen books, a humbling tally.[†]

I was always amazed, to use that word again, at how quickly he wrote. He could dash off a seven-hundred-word column in five minutes, about the length of time it took to type that many words. I would brag to people about how quickly my old man could write one of his columns, until one day he gently admonished me: "People *might*

---

[*]He wrote, all in all, fifty-six books; half a dozen of those were collections of columns and magazine work.

[†]Tom Wolfe once wrote a wonderful essay in *Esquire* in which he said that his favorite author, Balzac, wrote ninety novels; moreover, that Wolfe was convinced his idol was able to accomplish this feat because he lived before the advent of labor and time-saving devices.

get the impression I don't give them enough thought, and I do," he said. "I just happen to be a fast writer." He loved to relate a self-deflating anecdote of how he once told Gene Shalit, the extravagantly mustachioed and witty NBC-TV personality, that he had written a particular column in under five minutes. Shalit replied, "Yeah, I read that one."

When I was starting out as a professional writer myself, my awe of his speed began to mix with a certain amount of envy. For me, the words usually flowed at the speed of a glacier. Pup went every winter to Switzerland to write his books and would return six weeks later with a more or less complete manuscript. I won't make the posthumous claim for him that all his books are destined for literary immortality, but among those fifty are some real jewels, written in one and a half months—of *part-time* writing days.

In Switzerland, his routine was to spend mornings on correspondence and *National Review* and column writing, then lunch with Ken Galbraith or Niven or some exiled European king or czar or whomever on top of a mountain, have a glass or two of Fendant or Dôle wine, ski a few runs, then be back at his desk by four and write his book until seven. It took me the better part of a year—of eight-, ten-, fourteen-hour days, with no time off for hobnobbing with the Gstaadgratin—to crank out *my* first book. While I was writing it, over the garage apartment now inhabited by Danny, Pup and Mum embarked on a fourteen-day trip on a cruise ship from Rio to Panama. His plan was to start writing one of his sailing books on the voyage.* One midnight, lone and dreary, while I rewrote, glum and weary, won-

_____

Atlantic High. [1982]

dering if it was too late to apply to law school, my phone rang. It was the ship-to-shore operator, a call from Mr. Buckley. My pulse quickened. In those days, long-distance ship-to-shore calls were generally of a dire nature.

Christo?

Pup. Is everything . . . okay?

Guess what I did today?

What?

I finished my book! How's yours *coming? Ho, ho, ho!*

He'd written it in *twelve days*. I'm sure the "How's *yours* coming? Ho, ho ho!" was meant as a tease, but after congratulating him and hanging up, I spent some time staring at the .22-caliber rifle mounted on the wall, wondering if I could get the barrel in my mouth and pull the trigger with my big toe. Anyway, he wrote quickly, Pup, right up to the very end.

———

MOST AUTHORS ARE HAPPY—thrilled, even, to the point of doing cartwheels— upon finishing a book. But not Pup, not this time, for it left him, literally, without a reason to go on living. His depression deepened. I began to field alarmed phone calls and e-mails from his friends reporting that he sounded in low spirits.

He summoned me one afternoon to his bed and said to me, a look of near despair on his face, "Oh, Christo, I feel so fucking *awful*."

"I know you do, Pup," I said. "I know you do. I'm so sorry. I wish—"

"If it weren't for the religious aspect," he said, "I'd take a pill."

The religious aspect. Here we were venturing out onto thin ice. This was not the moment to break what remained of his heart by telling him that although I greatly admired the teachings of Jesus, I had long ago stopped believing that he had risen from the dead; it's an honest enough doubt, really, but one that rather undercuts the supernatural aspect of Christianity. At the same time, I was desperate to help put him out of his misery, if that was what he wanted. Misery it was. He missed Mum desperately.

This was a mystery to me. There had been so many rocky times. And yet I understood. He had depended on her for so long. Even when Mum wasn't speaking to him—which was about a third of the time—she looked after him: packing his bags, making sure he had everything he needed. "I'm just an Arab wife," she said (the quote appeared in her *New York Times* obituary). "When Bill says, 'Strike the tent,' I do." She had been brought up by a mother who inculcated in her daughters that their primary role in life was to take care of their men. Mum did that. She saw to every detail.

Even when Pup was despairing of

her behavior—as he did only occasionally—and sought refuge on the lecture circuit or wherever, he would call her every night, attempting reconciliation with, "Hi, Duck." "Duck" was the formal *vous* version of "Ducky," the word they called each other. If a transcript existed of their fifty-seven-year-long marriage and you did a computer quick-find search of "Ducky," you'd find 1,794,326.

When I shot the mock *60 Minutes* for their fortieth anniversary, their great British friend Peter Glenville[*] told the story on camera of one night at the dinner table in Stamford. Mum was furious with Pup for God knows what. Peter spoke in a velvety Oxford accent right out of *Brideshead Revisited*.

"And Bill said to her, 'Ducky—' She said, 'Don't call me "Ducky." ' Bill arched one of his eyebrows, perhaps both eye-

---

[*]Actor and theatrical and film director. He directed, among many other movies, *Becket*.

brows, and said, 'Oh. Why not?' She
said, 'I'm not going to go into it. Just
don't call me "Ducky." ' " And Bill said,
'Then what would you like me to call
you? Shitface?' "*

Peter followed that story by shifting
to a more somber tone and saying that
he had never in all his years known a
couple more loyal to each other. "If anyone ever said *anything* about him—a
lioness." Peter mimicked a paw in
midevisceration.

I experienced this loyalty from her
myself, and recalling it now, I cringe to
think of my presumption at her deathbed. (*I forgive you.*) Perhaps the most
memorable—certainly it was the most
public—occasion was in the late 1980s.
I'd written a lead review for the *New
York Times Book Review* of a biography of William S. Paley, founder of CBS.

------

*I suspect he actually said, "Shithead."

Mr. Paley, for all his achievements, was, in Sally Bedell Smith's able telling, a bit of a bounder in the human being department, and I had commented in the review approvingly of this portrait of a flawed man. Well, oh dear.

Shortly after the review appeared, there was a big dinner in New York at La Grenouille, the splendid commissary of le tout New York. A British aristocrat lady (they seem to abound in these pages) accosted Mum in full view of the crowded room with, "Your son is a *shit*." The lady was, *évidemment*, a spear carrier for the Paley camp. The room froze. And then Mum let her have it, with both paws. (I speak figuratively, of course, but it was apparently an electrifying moment.) This clash of doyennes became topic A in old New York for weeks. The society and gossip writers could barely keep up. At the time, I was safely on the high seas, crossing another (damned) ocean with Pup.

And now it occurs to me that I don't think I ever thanked her for taking up my cause. But that was Mum: When it came to protecting her men, she turned into Boadicea, Warrior Queen.

When Pup's sister Patricia first reported to her parents that her freshman Vassar roommate would be "perfect for Billy," the word she used to describe Mum was "regal." Regal Mum most absolutely was. Schuyler Chapin, in his eulogy to her at the Met, said, "She didn't enter a room, she took possession of it."

She was certainly regal in her proclivities and sensibilities. I remember one night arriving home at the apartment on Park Avenue to find her in a neck brace.

Mum, good Lord, what happened?

I was at a dinner last night and there was a—very—grand duchess present. I curtsied so low that I managed to catch my pearls on my heel

233

on the way up. It's a wonder I didn't garrote myself to death.

It's a cliché to say of anyone that they could have been on the stage, but I'll say it anyway: She'd have *killed*. Noel Coward or Moss Hart or Clare Boothe Luce would have loved to write lines for her. And she would have supplied some of her own bons mots. One night, watching one of the political conventions with her on TV, she said of someone giving a speech, "That woman is so stupid she ought to be *caged*." Another of her signature lines: "It is of an imbecility not to be credited." How—ever—did a "simple girl from the backwoods of British Columbia" learn to talk that way? When she and David Niven got going, you just stood back and went, *Wow.*

She took possession of it. Schuyler had it right. She took possession of her husband. And he was desolate now that she had gone. It was only now, seeing him so helpless without her, that I saw the extent of his devotion to her. The phrase *unconditional love* has always been an abstraction to me. Now I understand. I think he even missed her being cross with him.

HE MISSED, too, the roar of the crowd. That—I suspect—had been the reason for his skipping Jane's funeral to go get the award in Washington. He missed—everything: being able to breathe, being able to walk more than three feet without gasping. He was tired. He wanted to die. And I wanted to help him. I couldn't bear to see him suffer like this. But a voice within whispered, *For God's sake, don't end up in jail.*

I flash-forwarded through a deeply unpleasant film-at-eleven news segment, starring me, being arraigned for assisting suicide. I saw the district attorney stepping before the microphones. *We have found sufficient evidence to indict Christopher Buckley, son of conservative icon*—he'd be sure to put it that way—*William F. Buckley Jr.—for homicide.* On the bright side, maybe I'd get to spend some quality time with Michael Skakel.

The conversation proceeded:

Pup, I . . .

I struggled over how to put it, stuck between my inability to tell him that I simply didn't see "the religious aspect" as an impediment and my technical concern at being an accessory to suicide. But I'd learned the English language at the knee of one of its masters and, improvising, reached for the subjunctive.

Pup. Suppose, say, one were—accidentally—to ingest more than a, you know, prescribed *dosage of sleeping pills. Given your normal, say, high rate of ingestion, producing, as it does, a state of mental confusion . . . would that, really, qualify in the eyes of the*

Church as ... you know ... I mean, I'm hardly a priest, but still ...

He was propped up on his pillows, his eyes wandering sadly and philosophically into space. He looked at me with a flicker of the old wryness.

"I know what you're driving at," he said. We stared at each other. Neither of us spoke.

"Well," he said, "to be continued."

I left him to his nap, the religious aspect before us unresolved. As I passed through the sitting room, I glimpsed on a side table an advance copy of my current novel, *Boomsday* (*This one didn't work for me. Sorry. xxB*). I heard the district attorney add, *This crime is especially heinous given the fact that Christopher Buckley's new novel advocates mass suicide as a means of solving America's Social Security fiscal crisis.* Unfortunate coincidence, but—might be good for sales.

CHAPTER 13

I'd Do the Same for You

I was supposed to leave mid-July on a long-planned trip to California. One night as we watched the first of three—or was it four?—movies, he said apprehensively, "When are you leaving for California?"

"I'm not, Pup. I'm going to stay here with you."

He began to cry. I went over and pat-ted him on the back. He recovered his composure and said somewhat matter-of-factly, "Well, I'd do the same for you."

I smiled and thought, *Oh no, you wouldn't.* A year or two ago, I might have said it out loud, initiating one of our antler clashes. But watching him suffer had made my lingering re-sentments seem trivial and beside the point.

I had wondered, while keeping this vigil with him, whether to bring up certain things and talk them out so that when the end came, nothing would be left unsaid between us. But each time I hovered on the brink, I found myself shrugging and saying, *Let it go.* Perhaps it was another way of saying, as I had to Mum that night in the hospital, *I for-give you*, on the installment plan. I felt no need for what is called in other con-texts "the exit interview." I was able to love him now all the more and actually laugh (inwardly, anyway) at that "I'd do the same for you." Oh yeah? Ho, ho, ho.

When I was eleven, I spent three weeks in the hospital without a visit from him. True, he was on a trip to South Africa at the time, and in 1962, South Africa was a long way off. Still. When finally the doctors told Mum that I might not make it, she flashed word to him: *Come home.* And that he did, briskly, catching the next flight and changing planes—as he related proudly—in Nairobi, Cairo, Athens, Rome, Paris, London, and . . . Reykjavík! His absence from my sickbed was not any failure of love. It was, perhaps, just how it was in those days: The mothers took care of the children. By the time he arrived back, I was out of danger, and he brought with him spectacular presents: a leopard-skin rug, which he christened "King Kaiser" and whose head would serve as a gnaw bone to generations of Cavalier King Charles puppies; also a splendid ceremonial Wilkinson sword of the type, he said, carried by the guards at Buckingham Palace.

PUP'S LEGENDARY IMPATIENCE—a trait among the Great—could sometimes be, well, maddening. Ten minutes into my college graduation ceremony, he got bored and rounded up the family and friends in attendance and whisked them off to lunch at what we now call an "undisclosed location," leaving me to spend my graduation day wandering the campus in search of my family. I ended up having my graduation lunch alone, at the Yankee Doodle Diner. When I confronted him back home, grinding my back molars, he merely said airily, "I just assumed you had other plans." *Pup—on my graduation day?*

He could be a bit aloof that way. He could also be absentminded. When my mother went into labor with me, Pup and Uncle Firpo, Mum's brother, bundled her down the elevator at 444 East 57th, hailed a cab, got in, and drove off to the hospital, merrily chatting away; only after five or six blocks did they bother to notice that they had left her standing on the curb. She delighted in telling that story.

By the beginning of August, I had convalesced—if the verb can be used transitively—him back to some semblance of health. I'd been with him night and day since mid-June. Lucy reported that my fifteen-year-old son, Conor, had been reduced to looking me up on YouTube. I ached to be with him, yet I feared leaving Pup, sensing as I did that every time I left might be the last I saw him. But I had to get away, and I comforted myself knowing he would be looked after by the devoted Danny and a household staff of five. He would not be left to depend upon the mercy of strangers.

I woke early, bursting to go. Pup was still asleep, amid the doggies and a heap of crushed reading matter and the chugging oxygen machine. I kissed him, tiptoed out, and made it to our summer rental cabin in Maine in less than eight hours, where Conor and the Faithful Hound Jake were waiting for me in the little studio house. It felt like heaven. That night, to the smell of pine woods and the cry of loons, I e-mailed him.

Dear Pup, I don't know when you'll get this but I just wanted to say how much being with you these past weeks, despite the circumstances, has meant to me. I love you very much. Your devoted Christo.

He replied the next day, *OChristo, that note on TOP of everything you have done for me! XXXXp*

CHAPTER 14

Please Not to Arrest
My Dear Father

In September, his health deteriorating, Pup announced his intention to go back to the Mayo Clinic.

Why, Pup?

To find out what's wrong *with me.*

This was a bit of a conversation stopper, for by now it was pretty well established what was "wrong" with him: emphysema, diabetes, sleep apnea, skin cancer, heart disease, the usual prostate afflictions.

I didn't know what to say, other than a stammery, *Um, what is it you think they'll be able to do for you?*

Tell me how to get better.

It came out like a martini: six parts serious and one part wry. I nodded, *Well, why not?* Pup had always said, "Despair is a mortal sin," and though postreligious myself, I still admired the sentiment.* You don't want to tell someone who is dying (emphysema is progressive and incurable), *Forget it, you're toast.* At the same time, one doesn't want to hold out false hope.

The Mayo—venerable institution that it is—had a certain grim resonance in our household. In the early 1980s, David Niven had come to stay with

---

*As Winston Churchill said, "Never ever, ever, ever give up."

Mum and Pup in Stamford after receiving the definitive diagnosis there that he had Lou Gehrig's disease (amyotrophic lateral sclerosis).

David had been alarmed some months earlier by an appearance on *The Tonight Show* with Johnny Carson. David was one of the great raconteurs. He had told some very funny stories on the show, but that night after the taping, watching himself on TV in his hotel room, he was shocked by what he saw. He slurred his words and mumbled. He sounded *drunk*. The debility worsened, accompanied by other enfeeblements. Finally he took himself to Mayo, where he received the awful diagnosis. I remember Pup looking horrified as he told me that David had pressed the doctors to know what, exactly, would kill him in the end and was told: Suffocation. *You'll reach for a breath and eventually it won't be there.* This was a haunting memory for me now, given

Pup's increasing difficulty breathing. But, bowing to his wishes—one didn't *not* bow to Pup's wishes—we drove him to La Guardia one Sunday morning and put him on a plane for Rochester, where he would be met and taken to the clinic. He choked up when we said good-bye on the curb at the airport. I offered to go with him, but he said no.

The next morning, my phone rang: Julian, reporting that Pup had been found wandering around the lobby of the Mayo hotel in the middle of the night, "apparently a bit disorientated." I prepared to fly to Rochester; but by then Pup had announced that he had no further use for the Mayo and was on his way to the airport to come home. By the time he got back to Stamford, he was exhausted and physically depleted. I could barely make out what he was saying over the phone. He rallied a bit in the days following, but it was now clear that we were, as he often put it in other contexts, "approaching the point of diminishing returns."

Some years before, he'd gone off to Lourdes along with his friend William E. Simon, who'd been Nixon's secretary of the Treasury. The thought of these two—one a prominent political and journalistic figure, the other a captain of U.S. industry and former administrator of the world's biggest exchequer—carting lame and diseased pilgrims to and from the grotto where the Virgin Mary had allegedly appeared to a peasant girl is, well, humbling. One typically makes a pilgrimage to Lourdes for a special intention; Pup never vouchsafed to me what it was, but it was about the time I had declared my agnosticism, and I speculated whether he was petitioning Our Lady on my behalf.

When I was younger and periodically confessed to him my doubts about the One True Faith, he dealt with it in a fun and enterprising way: by taking me off to Mexico for four or five days, during which we would read aloud to each other from G. K. Chesterton's great work of Catholic apologetics, *Orthodoxy*.

Pup had been in the CIA in Mexico City in 1951. His boss there was E. Howard Hunt, who went on to . . . well, you know all about that. After dinner, Pup and I would walk around the city and he'd point out the various safe houses where he was to take refuge in the event of "being blown." (As a teenager, I was enchanted by this coinage.) Mexico City had been a pretty hot spot back during the cold war. It was here that Trotsky was pickaxed through the skull by Stalin's agent; here that Lee Harvey Oswald had applied to the Soviets for a visa. And it had been here, too, in Mexico City between 1905 and 1921 that Pup's father, William F. Buckley Sr., had had his great adventures as a lawyer and oil wildcatter. Living in Mexico between those dates was roughly the equivalent of living in Paris between 1789 and 1801, and my grandfather was right in the thick of it. He'd talked Pancho Villa out of shooting a train conductor; was kidnapped by thugs hired by competitors and taken into a forest to be killed. When U.S. Marines bombarded Vera Cruz, they asked him to serve as governor-civil of the city. He refused indignantly, disgusted as he was by Woodrow Wilson's interventionism. Later, the Mexican government paid him the compliment of asking him to represent it at the ABC conference in Niagara. He made a fortune in oil there, only to have it confiscated by a subsequent government.

So we Buckleys had history down here, and it was delicious to inhale it as I walked along dark *calles* and *avenidas* with Pup as he pointed out his cloak-and-dagger locales. The next morning, we'd drive up into the hills of Cuernavaca and Taxco and sit on narrow balconies overlooking the *zócalos*, drinking margaritas and reading Chesterton aloud to each other. Not a bad way to restore one's faith, really.* Four or five days of this and I was content to shrug off my doubts about the Immaculate Conception or the Trinity. They were some of the best days I ever had with him. In one of the last conversations we had before he died, we smiled at the memory of what we always called "the most amazing meal we ever had"—at a roadside stand in Taxco, a cheese-and-chicken tortilla washed down with an ice cold bottle of Bohemia beer. Cost: one dollar.

---

*It sure beat the you-know-what out of the annual retreats I'd experienced at boarding school, where they would bring in army drill instructor–type priests who yelled at us that whacking off to *Playboy* centerfolds was a guarantee of going to hell and that for some of us, it might already be too late.

251

A MONTH AFTER THE MAYO EPISODE, I
came to Stamford for Thanksgiving. Our
annual ritual was to drive up to Sharon,
the town in northwestern Connecticut where Pup had grown up with his
nine brothers and sisters. I have an early
memory of one of those drives. I might
have been five or six. Pup may have been
the only human left on the planet to use
WordStar, but he had always been a gad-
get freak, and on this November day in
1957, there was between us on the front
seat of the diesel Mercedes an enormous reel-to-reel tape recorder, playing
a recording of *Macbeth*. I could make no
sense of it whatsoever, and what little
I did understand sounded pretty grim.
Pup explained the story. When Lady
Macbeth started going on about not being able to get her hands clean, I asked
why didn't she just try Palmolive? And
so began my tutelage with the world's
coolest mentor.

Over the next fifty years, we had

some of our best talks on those drives up to Sharon. The November sun was usually far down in the sky by the time we would set off. There's something to be said for long drives in the dark. They seem to enable candor. It's cozy, and you're not looking into each other's eyes. *As a matter of fact, Pup, I've taken LSD on a number of occasions, and you know, it's really quite amazing.* Try saying that to your dad, when you're age twenty, across a brightly lit dinner table, with Mom looking on, wide-eyed.

I'd been looking forward to it this year. I sensed that it would probably be our last Thanksgiving drive up to Sharon. I'd brought Caitlin along. Pup doted on what he called "my favorite granddaughter." (He had only one.) I'd warned Cat that driving with Pup now often involved a tendency that she might find a bit unusual—namely, his habit of opening the front door while the car was moving, and peeing. He did this routinely now, including from his limousine, in traffic. I've often wondered if there are people out there scratching their heads and saying, *Marge—was that William F. Buckley Jr. who just peed on our Lexus?* If you're out there, the answer is, yes, you were selected from among thousands of other motorists on I-95 to be tinkled on by the Lion of the Right. You should feel honored. Caitlin, being a nineteen-year-old of sensitivity, was naturally horrified by this prospect; but, understanding that Pup was "not himself," she agreed that in this dire eventuality, she would keep silent and slink low in the backseat.

Embarrassing One's Young is in some ways the entire *point* of having children. I discovered the joy myself when Cat was perhaps three years old and I did something (a public burp) that caused her to turn crimson with shame and to renounce all consanguinity with me. In addition to making me fiercely proud of him over the years, Pup provided a number of *Beam me up, Scotty* moments, and the role his prostate played in the occasions of filial mortification must not go uncelebrated.

It's possible that his utter casualness in the field of public urination stemmed from a lifetime of peeing off the side of his sailboats. (There are two places where a man can really *be a man*: at sea and in the woods.) But afflicted as he was by the prostate conditions that seem to account for 95 percent of TV advertising during the evening news, Pup disdained normal conveniences and instead opted for what in the Watergate era was called a "modified, limited, hang-out option."

One time, on a father-son visit to Montreal, he announced that he had just received a flash priority message from Bladder Command. Given that we were standing in front of the city's main church, my own sphincter tightened at what I feared might ensue. I suggested that we would certainly find a loo just around the cor— But no, already he was wending his way, unzippingly, to the side of the Notre-Dame basilica. *Oh, no.* We were not alone—indeed, there were hundreds of Montrealers in attendance, no doubt many of them devout Catholics. I hastily cinched my scarf about my face so that I was no more recognizable than Omar Sharif in his opening scene in *Lawrence of Arabia* and made my own way hastily in an opposite direction, meanwhile rehearsing my French for *Respected and handsome Gendarme, please not to arrest my dear father, who is a grand personage in our French-loving country of America and, to be sure, a Knight of Malta. He is most vocal in his opinion that Quebec should be allowed to separate from the hateful, English-speaking government of Ottawa. If you would kindly direct us to a Protestant church, he will be pleased to urinate on it instead!* It was always an adventure with Pup.

But not this time, for when Cat and I arrived, he greeted us in his garage study and said, sadly, that he was too ill to make it. So we had Thanksgiving in Stamford and on Saturday celebrated his eighty-second birthday, along with his best friend, Van Galbraith, and our neighbor Jimmy Edgerton. Jimmy, now eighty-eight years old, had grown up on Wallack's Point and told of having been in this room, our dining room where we sat, in the 1920s. Van, once bulldog-athletic, had undergone thirty radiation treatments for cancer in the previous month. He could barely walk. Pup, Van, and Jimmy, handsome Yalies all. Within six months, they would all be dead.

———

*We will serenade our Louie, while
life and voice shall last,
Then we'll pass and be forgotten
with the rest.*

I'D FOUND PUP A RENTAL HOUSE in Fort Lauderdale for December–January, where he could repair with his latest amanuensis/protégé and write his new book, a memoir of his friendship with Ronald Reagan.

Having a new project had lifted Pup's spirits, as had the prospect of being near his old friend Carl Wohlenberg. Carl and Pup had formed a lifelong friendship one day at Yale in 1946, when, at the end of the first lecture in freshman physics, the professor had said, "I assume there are no questions." There were two bursts of hysterical laughter from opposite ends of the auditorium. Pup and Carl had found each other.

Julian and Danny were tasked with conveying Pup's equipage there from Stamford: his complicated array of computers, which took up about as much space as the original ENIAC; his books; music machines; vast trove of CDs; breathing machines; doggies. Pup did not travel light. His and Mum's annual departures for Switzerland were a mirth-rich anecdotal environment. They would present themselves at the Swissair check-in counter with enough bags to fill the entire hold of a C-5A Galaxy, along with at least three dogs, including a malevolent Pekingese named Foo. At which point Pup would deploy full-frontal WFB situational charm.

So, Monsieur Buckley, we have today, oof . . . eighteen baggages? In addition to the dogs?

Is it that many? Heavens. Ha, ha. Well [eyes twinkling] I would never disagree with a Swiss on the matter

of accuracy, especially as my own an-
cestors were Swiss. Ha, ha. . . .*

At the end of the negotiation, Pup
would have bargained Swissair down
to charging him for only one extra
bag and one malevolent Pekingese. He
would relate his victories in the field
of excess baggage surcharge with the
pride of a general who had just turned
back a German tank offensive.

It was during those forty-odd winters
in Switzerland that Mum and Pup were,
perhaps, their best selves together. For
a quarter century of those years, they
rented a château in Rougemont, near
Gstaad—a tenth-century castle at the
foot of a tall alp called the Videmanette.
Pup wrote his books, and Mum turned
the pile of stones into a salon. Everyone came. After one of Julian's excel-

---

*Pup's mother's maiden name was Steiner. Her
grandfather, a boot maker, had immigrated to New
Orleans from the canton of St. Gallen.

lent dinners, they and the guests would descend to the ground floor, where a painting atelier had been set up. In one photo, you can see Dame Rebecca West slapping paint onto a canvas alongside Princess Grace. There's even a photo of Teddy Kennedy and Pup painting together. At evening's end, he asked if he could borrow a car to drive himself back to Gstaad. Mum shouted out, "Don't give him one—there are two bridges between here and Gstaad!"

In almost every photo taken during the painting sessions, you can see David Niven, wearing his smock, painting seriously. He was good. Marc Chagall dropped by one night. Pup—he told this story with appropriate mortification—showed him one of his paintings. Chagall remarked, *"Pauvre peinture!"* (Poor paint!) Ken and Kitty Galbraith, Greek shipping magnates, various Romanovs, Charlie Chaplin, Nabokov, James Clavell, German *Grafs*, a Danish queen, King Constantine of Greece, Spanish ministers, English swells, Oxford dons, Swiss art dealers, the whole jumbo jet set—they all came to Mum and Pup's château to be wined and fed and laugh. (In addition, that is, to the painting.) It was there, perhaps more than in New York and Stamford, that I saw most close up the binary energy that the two of them put out. People just wanted to be around them. They were the fun Americans: the cool intellectual who wrote spy novels on the side and his beautiful, witty, outrageous wife. They had—how to put it?—class.

One night, as they were getting ready for dinner, a chimney fire broke out and swiftly consumed the entire château. The Rougemont fire department arrived late, and drunk, and unable to cope. Mum lost everything, including her recently deceased mother's jewels. Pup organized a sort of bucket brigade to rescue his book-in-progress and office library. David and

Hjordis Niven, driving to dinner there from the town where they lived, noticed an orange glow as they approached and wondered, *What could that be?* Another guest, the painter Raymond de Botton, driving from the other direction, also noticed a glow above Rougemont. I still have the painting that he did of it. It's called *Château Brûlée*. No one was hurt, but Mum went into a bad depression. Jerry Zipkin, staying in Paris, went out and bought her an entire new wardrobe and arrived on the train from Montreux bearing a zillion shopping bags.

The immolation was the second trauma of their Swiss days. In 1965, Mum broke her leg skiing—broke it badly. The bone splintered into a dozen pieces. The plate the surgeons installed was a foot long and contained dozens of screws. The X-ray of it, which I have just tossed into a Dumpster, looks like something they study in med school. She was on crutches for two years. The surgeon who did the operation became a friend. He was an avid mountaineer and many years later froze to death alone on a mountain after falling.

The last time I visited them in Switzerland, in 2000, Pup called me a few days before I was to arrive to say that he wanted to visit Auschwitz. He was writing a novel about the Nuremberg trials and needed to see it for himself. So we went, and my last memory of seeing Mum and Pup amid the beau monde of Gstaad is a confused one, mingled with images of the worst place on earth.

WORD CAME BACK from Fort Lauderdale that Julian and the first installment of WFB tonnage had arrived, but with the sad news that Sebbie, Pup's devoted eight-year-old Cavalier and bedside defender, had suffered a heart attack on the way down and died.

CHAPTER 15

Blood of the Fathers

I would get reports from Julian and Danilo on how it was going down in Florida. There were good days and not-so-good days, the not-so-good days often following not-so-good nights, when Pup, frustrated at finding himself awake at three a.m., would reach for a fistful of sleeping pills. By this point,

I found myself hoping that one night he would accidentally overdose. There was no guilt to the thought. I wanted him out of pain.

Pup revealed to me, in an unusually legibly typed e-mail, that he'd discussed the religious aspect with a local doctor—"*un Católico*" (a Catholic), he pointed out. The e-mail revealed nothing more, and I did not press. I wondered how their conversation would have gone. Lots of subjunctive, I should think, on Pup's part, a lot of lawyerly subordinate clauses: *Were one, say, to ingest a specific number of Stilnoxes . . . might that, under certain circumstances, bring about the necessary diminution of pulmonary functionality so as to frustrate, say, the cardiological imperatives?* Tonight's guest on *Firing Line*—Dr. Jack Kevorkian.

In other news, he was back to writing his column, and I rejoiced at that. Since 1962, his whole work metabolism had been set to the rhythm of the column. One particular column he wrote in Florida was, I thought, especially good, and I sent him a filial e-mail pat on the back, telling how proud I was of him that he could still muster the old skills. He responded instantly, and I could feel him glowing through the computer screen. Toward the end of his life, Joseph Conrad, grumpy over a bad review, said at the table with admirable ingenuousness—not always a trait in evidence among great writers: "I don't want criticism. I want *praise*."

One night—it would have been 1974 or 1975—before Pup launched twin new careers as a writer of sailing books and Blackford Oakes novels (both genres propelled him to the top of the bestseller lists), he was gloomy over a recent thrashing he'd taken from *The New York Times Book Review*. Pup was no stranger to bad reviews. Reviewing his first book, McGeorge Bundy, speaking for the Establishment, called him, among other unpleasant things, "a twisted young man." And he'd been called far worse over the years. But after this umpteenth consecutive drubbing by the newspaper of record, he was hurting. As we sat in the sunroom at Wallack's Point, he said to me, "They might at least say that I write well." Some criticism did amuse him. Up until it changed ownership, *Kirkus Reviews* gave a hostile review to every single one of his books. Around our house, Mrs. Kirkus was referred to as "that-bitch-Virginia-Kirkus."

He did, certainly, like praise. *Not* unusual in writers, but Pup had developed certain—shall we say—Conradian aspects in his declining years. During the posthospital convalescence, he would have me read to him e-mail "William F. Buckley" news alerts that he'd programmed Google to send him. There were mentions in cyberspace of "William F. Buckley" about every three seconds. By the time I'd read the one hundredth or so out loud to him, this had become a somewhat vexing aspect of my nursing shifts. I would come to groan upon opening his e-mail to see seventy-five WFB news alerts.

I called him in Florida one day. He sounded very down and said that he was having a "rough time" with his Reagan book. My eyes watered. I thought, *Jesus. Eighty-two years old, founder of a political movement, author of over fifty books, nothing left to prove, barely able to breathe, and still beating himself over the head because the writing's not going well.*

He kept at it, and that book, his last, is going to press now as I write this. The first chapter ends with a speech he gave in 1985, in President Reagan's presence, at the thirtieth-anniversary dinner of *National Review.* He addressed it directly to his old friend. It ends:

As an individual you incarnate American ideals at many levels. As the final responsible authority, in any hour of great challenge, we depend on you. I was nineteen years old when the bomb went off over Hiroshima, and last week I turned 60. During the interval I have lived a free man in a free and sovereign country, and this only because we have husbanded a nuclear deterrent, and made clear our disposition to use it if necessary. I pray that my son, when he is 60, and your son, when he is 60, and the sons and daughters of our guests tonight will live in a world from which the great ugliness that has scarred our century has passed. Enjoying their freedoms, they will be grateful that, at the threatened nightfall, the blood of their fathers ran strong.

His fifty-sixth and, given that he died while writing it, one might suppose, final book. I put it this way not to be coy, but because there seems to be a possibility, given enthusiasm in various publishing quarters, of bringing out another collection of his articles. So this might turn out not to be his last book. His book on Barry Goldwater has just come out. One month before, another book, a collection of his "Notes and Asides" from *National Review,* appeared under the really great title *Cancel Your Own Goddam Subscription.* And here came yet another in the pipeline. Pup wrote more books dead than some authors do alive.

That his last book would be about Reagan struck me as a natural coda to his oeuvre, inasmuch as WFB was the founder and primum mobile of the movement that eventually put Reagan in the White House. As it's been said more than once: If it hadn't been for Buckley, there mightn't have been Goldwater, and without Goldwater, there mightn't have been Reagan.

Ronald Reagan was an elusive personality. His biographer Edmund Morris found him so elusive that he resorted, in his masterful but certainly controversial book *Dutch,* to confect a fictional character, simply in an effort to deconstruct his subject. But though Reagan tended famously to shy from intimacy, I think it's possible that Pup may have gotten as close to him as any friend could. It certainly *was* a friendship. WFB was very close to Nancy Reagan, as the letters in the book attest. At various points, Pup became a mentor (that ghastly word again) to the Reagan children, Patti and Ron Jr.

I first met Reagan when Pup took me along with him to California in 1966 to do several *Firing Line* tapings. Honesty compels me to say that for this fourteen-year-old, the real excitement of the trip was the *Firing Line* taping not with the new governor of California, but with Robert Vaughn, star of *The Man from U.N.C.L.E.* Vaughn was at the time an aspirant liberal eminence, which vocation turned out to be short-lived.

The Reagans gave a cocktail party for Pup at the governor's mansion. Le tout Sacramento turned out. I was swiftly ignored amid the sea of grown-ups and wandered out into the garden and sat down by myself. A few moments later, I sensed the presence of someone next to me and, turning, saw the governor of California looming large and movie-star handsome in a white jacket. He had seen me go off by myself and, sensing that I must be feeling lost and out of place, had left his guests to come and talk. I never forgot that. If Reagan was capable of reticence, he was also capable of graciousness. He was a gentleman. In that capacity, he and WFB were made for each other.

Fifteen years later, quite by accident (I'd written something in *Esquire* that had impressed Vice President George Bush's press secretary), I found myself working in Ronald Reagan's White House. The Reagans kindly invited me to the odd social occasion. At one of these, I nearly caused a faux pas of national proportion.

The invitation was for dinner in the residence upstairs and a movie afterward. I had a big speech to write for Bush that night and pleaded urgently with Muffie Brandon, Mrs. Reagan's social secretary, to be excused from the movie. She *tsk-tsk*ed but said all right, but that I must be discreet about leaving. I said of course. As I made my stealthy exit just before the lights went down in the family theater, I rounded a corner in the hallway and bumped smack into—Ronald Reagan, returning either from the men's room or from ordering a richly deserved missile strike on some Middle Eastern despot.

He smiled that thousand-watt smile and regarded me curiously.

"Where are you going?" he said. "We're about to start the movie."

"Um," I said, dissembling, "just going to the men's room, Mr. President. I'll be right there. Go ahead and start without me."

He smiled and went off, phalanxed by Secret Service, including Tim McCarthy, who a few months earlier had interposed himself between the president and John Hinckley, taking a .22 slug in the chest.

I made my way down the long corridor in the basement and was about to exit the White House when I heard behind me a sibilant and frantic, *"Psssst!"*

Looking back, I saw Muffie Brandon gesticulating urgently.

"He just announced to everyone

that we weren't going to start without you."

Oh dear. I skulked back, Muffie more or less leading me by the ear, to find fifty guests glowering at me and my seat saved—in the front row, next to the president and Mrs. Reagan.

I experienced many such acts of grace and favor during my time at the White House. Looking back on it, I realize—not that I didn't at the time—that these were reciprocations for the kindnesses Pup had shown to the Reagan children.

A few years later, in 1985, I found myself—again, accidentally—ghostwriting David Stockman's memoirs, under furious deadline pressure. (I use the term *ghostwriting* in the narrow, technical sense: My job was to turn a mountain—yea, a veritable Kilimanjaro—of manuscript into readable English.) There was a piquancy to this assignment, inasmuch as David Stockman had become famous mainly for an act of impertinence to Reagan while serving as his budget director. But a) Stockman's beef was about policy, not in any way ad hominem against Reagan; and, well, b) I needed the dough.

In the midst of this death march fell *National Review*'s gala thirtieth-anniversary dinner at the Plaza in New York. I pleaded with Pup that I couldn't attend—I barely had time to eat meals. *No*, he insisted, *you have to be there*, as he put it somewhat mysteriously, *for reasons that will become apparent*. I grumpily assented. Pup wasn't someone to whom you could say no.

So I went and was seated right above the podium when he gave the speech that is reproduced here. Looking back on that moment, on those two amazing men, I reflect that, yes, the blood of the fathers truly did run strong.

CHAPTER 16

That Would Be a Real Bore

The lease on the Fort Lauderdale house was up mid-January, but with the Reagan book still unfinished, and January in Connecticut being January in Connecticut, I tried to persuade Pup to remain in Florida. But he was adamant about coming home, and I suspect now that he was coming home to die. With all due respect to the Sunshine State, when my time comes, I shouldn't want to die there, either. I can see spending some of my senescence there, but I shouldn't want the Reaper to find me on the golf course or in a condo. "I want death . . . to find me planting my cabbages," wrote Michel de Montaigne. But to die in, say, Fort Lauderdale . . . there seems something—as Pup would say—*contra naturam* about that. In *The Importance of Being Earnest*, the Reverend Chasuble, informed that so-and-so died in Paris, tut-tuts: "In Paris? I fear that does not point, at the end, to a very serious state of mind."* New Englanders, growing up as we do with hot summer fields and frozen-over ponds, are hardwired to the seasons. Now it

---

*Ironic and sad to reflect that Wilde himself would die in Paris, in wretched circumstances, five years after writing that line.

was winter in Connecticut, and I think Pup wanted to be back on native soil when it happened. It was time.

Time for someone else, too: his great friend Van Galbraith. They'd met on election day 1948, in New Haven. Best friends for six decades. They'd sailed across three oceans together (I was along); had seen each other through tragedies. Van's were particularly awful: the loss of two daughters, one a little girl named Julie, age six.* Pup had maneuvered Van's appointment as Reagan's U.S. ambassador to France. Van— Ohio born, handsome, blond, brawny, broken-nosed, Yale football player, navy officer, CIA man, and Wall Street banker—was a gleeful cold warrior and a most unusual diplomat. He gave

---

*Her headstone contains one of the loveliest inscriptions I know: *Elle est venue, elle a sourit, elle est parti.* (She came, she smiled, she left.)

François Mitterrand's Socialist government more heartburn than a dozen escargots. *Did you see what Van did yesterday? It's all* over *the news. Boy, oh boy, Shultz is going to recall his ass, he keeps this up.* Van's tenure in Paris was *An American in Paris* meets *Day of the Jackal.* He had the rare gift of being able to make almost any unpleasant situation funny. He was certainly the only person you could forgive for waking you in the middle of the ocean at two in the morning to go stand watch. *Christo, good news. You don't have to be asleep anymore.* I loved him. Everyone did. I've not yet lost a best friend to death. I could only imagine what losing him meant to Pup.

HE CAME HOME. I started at his appearance. He could barely walk now. The breathing had worsened to the point where he would attach the oxygen tube to his nostrils without any preliminary Socratic dialogue about whether oxygen actually made a difference. At table, he'd hunch forward over his food and fall asleep. We'd get him upstairs, and then just as I was going to sleep, the intercom would buzz. He'd like a chocolate milkshake. So that would be made and brought, and having finished that, he wanted a beer. And after that, peanut brittle. I wondered, administering these surely lethal midnight snacks to a diabetic, whether this would be sufficient to send me off to jail. *We have evidence that Christopher Buckley did knowingly provide chocolate milkshakes and beer to the late conservative icon William F. Buckley. . . .*

"Pup, do you think you ought to be having all this quite so late at night? I mean, with the diabetes and all . . ."

"It's delicious. Have some."

[Patting my own protuberant belly in hopes that self-deprecation might inspire moderation on his part.] "Oh, no, no. Ha. Look at me. Jabba the Hutt."

"Who?"

"The grotesquely fat alien in . . ." Never mind.

"Now," he would say brightly, "what I would like, more than anything in the world, is a milk rum punch."

We find the defendant, Christopher Buckley, guilty.

In the 1950s, Mum and Pup would hold the *National Review* Christmas office party in Stamford. Pup would make milk rum punch. I used to help him. Never one to waste time, Pup kept to a simple recipe: one quart milk, one quart rum, one quart ice cream. He might, just for the heck of it, empty an entire (large) bottle of vanilla extract into it. The effects of this milky elixir upon the conservative movement were quite galvanizing. Pup would play Handel's *Messiah* at full blast on the phonograph. By the time the final joyous hallelujah trumpet blasts sounded, the entire conservative movement was passed out, comatose. The wonder is any of them made it home alive. How different history might have been.

He had begun to do odd things, like getting up at two in the morning, dragging himself to the shower, getting dressed, ringing poor Julian, and asking for breakfast to be brought. Julian, as demure and accommodating a soul as has ever lived, never thought to say to His Lordship, *It is two in the morning, Mr. Buckley, but if you would like breakfast, I can certainly bring it.* These scenes had a certain comic aspect to them, for Pup, having had his brekkers and declaring his intention to go to the garage study, would then look out into the darkness and see that it was now three a.m.

Except that it wasn't really funny. One night, sleeping in my room down the hall, I heard a sound and went in.

That Would Be a Real Bore

He was sitting cross-legged in front of the TV cable box and DVD player. The server of his computer, one of those heavy floor units, was knocked over, along with his chair. His wrist was swollen, the skin broken. It was sub-arctic. He'd lowered the AC to fifty-two degrees. His hands were roaming over the DVD player and cable box buttons.

"Pup—what are doing?"

"Trying to make it *warmer*."

I managed to haul him back into bed and get him covered.

"Oh, thank you. *Thank you.* That's so much *better*."

We took him to the emergency room the next day; the wrist was broken. He had no memory of the night before. None. So it was time for the lecture.

Pup, I'm worried that the next time, it's going to be your hip or your pelvis or something like that. And if that happens, well, I don't need to spell it out, but that would be a real bore.

I was choosing my words carefully. Pup used the word *bore* where others might use *catastrophe* or *calamity* or even *tragedy of earthshaking dimensions*. If *shee-it* was his augmented word chord, *bore* was its diminished counterpart. Once, crossing an ocean in a sailboat, we ran out of water a thousand miles from landfall, causing him to observe that the situation was "a bit of a bore." If you, too, have ever brushed your teeth with orange Fanta, you may agree.

Whenever he added the intensifier *real* or *bloody* (he'd learned English, his third language, at age six in school in London), the subject at hand might be either a mass outbreak of the ebola virus or an imminent Soviet nuclear attack. So I thought that "real bore" might convey "months in some rehab unit with Nurse Ratched and no midnight milkshakes and beer."

He stared and said, "Yes, that *would* be a real bore."

But then a night or two later, there was another crashing sound—a loud one—and I had to cantilever him back into bed. It was clear that the era of day and night nurses was approaching. (I had dismissed them earlier on.) And that was problematic, for once nurses were introduced, it would be impossible for Danny and me to help him end his suffering, if he indicated to us that he wanted that. A year into keeping vigil with him, watching him suffer, Danny and I were growing desperate. We talked about scenarios.

I told Dan about a movie I'd seen called *Igby Goes Down*, in which two young sons of a terminally ill woman (brilliantly played by Susan Sarandon) help her to die. They give her ice cream laced with sleeping pills and then, once she passes out, put a plastic bag over her head. Wrenching as the scene is, there's a poignant, almost comical moment as through the plastic bag they see her eyes suddenly pop open, causing the boys to jump. In discussing this, Danny and I felt like some Ebert and Roeper broadcast from hell. I found myself wondering grimly, *Am I really going to take my cue from a movie written by Gore Vidal's nephew?* In the end, thank God—an expression I still find myself using—it was moot.

CHAPTER 17

Boy, How He'd Have Loved This

At nine-thirty the morning of February 27, my son's sixteenth birthday, my cell phone rang in Washington. Julian.

"Hello, Christopher. I'm sorry to disturb you, but there's been an emergency."

He'd found Pup on the floor of his

garage study. The ambulance had been called. I said without even thinking, "Get the bracelet on him" (the DNR bracelet).

I don't know the technical definition of shock, but after hanging up with Julian, I found myself wandering around the house aimlessly, thinking that I should go on with what I'd been doing—my income taxes. *Maybe if I do them, this won't have happened.* My thinking was as jumbled as the verb tenses in that sentence. I waited five minutes and called the house. Julia, the maid, answered. She was sobbing, a kind of wailing sound. *"Oh, Christobal, Christobal. Venga. Venga."* (Christopher, come.) So, that was that. I knew. Pup was gone.

Julian came on. "The police are here and would like to have a word, if they might."

An Officer James came on. He said, "I'm sorry for your loss." I thanked him.

He said they had to wait for the medical examiner to arrive, "just to make sure there was no foul play involved." I thought how archaic that sounded. *Foul play,* as if I'd wandered onto the set of an Agatha Christie play.

I said, "He's been very ill."

Officer James said, "Yes, I understand that. Where are you, may I ask?" Washington, I said. "Oh," he said, as if I were no longer a suspect. "In . . . *Washington.*"

"Yes," I said.

He asked if I had a specific funeral home in mind. I said yes, nearly adding that we were regular customers at Leo P. Gallagher, up on Summer Street. Julian came back on, and I told him to stay with Pup.

I walked about the house, conducting a kind of conversation with myself. *Okay, so that's that. Should we . . . do the taxes? No, we're not going to do the taxes now. Okay, so what* do *we do, then?* I leaned my forehead against a wall and took some deep breaths. I felt underwater.

My instincts said, *Get to the body, get in the car, and drive to Stamford.* (Five hours up I-95.) But it was Conor's sixteenth birthday. I'd promised him a driving lesson that day after school. One of Pup's favorite mantras—though he did sometimes take liberties with it as an excuse not to do something he didn't want to do—was: "Life goes on." Another was "Where there are no alternatives, there are no problems." I realized I was crying now, so I blotted my eyes with toilet paper, sucked in a few more deep breaths, and said, *Okay, come on, get a grip. Time to grow up.* At age fifty-five, this is a perfectly reasonable request to make of yourself, and indeed, it is a very major component of orphanhood. *Phone calls. You have to make the phone calls.*

So I placed my calls, first to family.
I said the same thing to them all: "I'm
calling with some sad news." It's effi-
cient; you almost don't need to say anything more. I called Henry Kissinger.
He wept. I went down my list. I made
my calls. I called my friend John Tierney at *The New York Times* and asked
him to alert the obit desk. I sent out an
e-mail: "My father died this morning at
9:30, at his desk, in his study, in Stamford." I added:

> *Take him all in all, Horatio, he was
>   a man.*
> *I shall not look upon his like again.*

I got it slightly wrong and later re-
buked myself for not having looked up
the correct wording.

The phone began to ring. My doctor, married to a White House television correspondent, called: "They just
announced it from the White House."

A few minutes later, the phone rang again. "Mr. Buckley, I have the president for you." I assumed it was President Bush 41, but no, it was his son. It was a gracious gesture, especially given some of the things I had written about his administration.

He was quite a guy.

Yes, sir, he was.

I started to choke up. I thought of his father's "Bawl Brigade." I really didn't want to lose it over the phone with the president of the United States—*grow up!*—so I jujitsued the conversation into a different tone and told the president that he'd died at his desk.

You might say he died with his boots on, sir. A Texan like yourself would appreciate that. He laughed at that and said, yes, that was a good way to go.

God bless you.

God bless you, too, sir. Thank you for calling.

Chris Matthews called.

He was such *a great guy*. Chris was very fond of my father and had continued to have him on his show *Hardball*, perhaps past the point where Pup should have declined. In one episode I'd watched, taped in Pup's study, he kept leaning back in his Aeron chair, at points entirely disappearing from camera view, with the result that his appearance became a kind of *Where's Waldo?* It was sort of funny. Chris had said more than once that Pup was "one of the reasons I went *into* politics in the first place."

The phone rang. It's strange, who calls. You don't hear from people you expect to hear from; and you hear from people you'd never expect to hear from. It was Larry Gelbart calling. We hadn't spoken in maybe a dozen years. He'd reviewed *Thank You for Smoking* for *The New York Times*. He's slightly more famous for having written, among other classics, *Tootsie* and *A Funny Thing*

Happened on the Way to the Forum. I remembered that his father was a barber and cut his hair.

I don't suppose your *dad is still. . . .*

Oh yeah. He's still going strong. Well, listen, just wanted to call and give you a hug.

Doug Martin of the *Times* called. He was gentle but professional. He needed the precise cause of death. I said, "Old age, Doug." He said that wasn't quite up to *New York Times* standards of precision. I said we were still waiting for the medical examiner to arrive. Doug's obituary, prepared in advance, could be studied in obituary-writing classes at journalism school. It was up on the *Times* Web site by 11:04 a.m.

My e-mail in-box filled. My desk phone became a switchboard. NPR, AP, the *Chicago Tribune, Los Angeles Times, Newsweek.* So I was press secretary now. There was no avoiding it. It was news and, it appeared, big news. I thought with a smile, *Boy, how he'd have loved this, the mother of all WFB Google news alerts.*

It was a long day. Conor and I had our driving lesson, and that night we went ahead with the surprise birthday party Lucy had arranged with his friends. *Life goes on.* Sixteen years ago, I'd called Pup in Switzerland to tell him that he had a grandson, and he'd cried. Today I got a call, and I cried. *Grandfather dies, father dies . . . you're next.*

After his friends left, Conor and I watched a movie I'd happened to order from Netflix called *Death at a Funeral*: a black English comedy about a dysfunctional family holding a funeral at home for the dad, who, it transpires, had been conducting a homosexual affair with a dwarf. It's very funny. I can't quite explain why we watched such a movie on this night or why we found it so funny. Life goes on. I said, *Well, Boog* (my nickname for him), *here's hoping Pup's funeral won't be quite as exciting.*

CHAPTER 18

He's Looking Much Better

I drove to Stamford the next morning. I didn't want to sit on the train blubbering and blowing my nose in the Quiet Car, disturbing the peace of my fellow Amtrak passengers. There's something, too, to be said for a long, solitary drive—it concentrates the mind. By Baltimore, mine was

concentrated to the point of calling Pitts
to say that I'd decided to bury Pup in
Sharon. She was delighted, though this
wasn't at all what Pup had specified. But
having made the decision, I felt—for the
first time in my life—entirely indepen-
dent of paternal authority or rebuke.

Years ago, Pup commissioned a
large bronze crucifix from the Connecticut sculptor Jimmy Knowles. It's
a beautiful piece of modern art. He
placed it in the middle of the lawn
in Stamford, to a distinct grumbling
from Mum, who viewed her garden as
off-limits to my father's artistic (and in
this case overtly religious) intrusions.
Mum's ashes were now inside the
cross, in a heavy brass canister that
looked as if it had been designed as
a container of plutonium. Pup's wish
was that he, too, be cremated and join
her in the cross. The idea of Mum,
who wasn't all that religious, encased
for all eternity inside Pup's crucifix

had afforded the two of us a few grim chuckles over the years. "Just sprinkle me in the garden or send me out with the trash. I most certainly do not wish to be inside that *object*." But she went first, so that was that.

Pup expected me to keep the Stamford house, but beautiful as it was and fond though (most of) my memories were, it was expensive, and after death taxes, I seriously doubted I would be able to maintain it. But not wanting to hurt his feelings, I went along with the fiction that I would keep it. This, however, left me with a conundrum: what to do with the cross. I tippytoed into this minefield one evening over our martinis.

"Say, Pup, I know you want your ashes in the cross . . ."

"I *absolutely* want them in the cross," he said in a preemptive tone of voice.

"Right. Right. I was only thinking, what if, you know, the house, if I, well, you never *know* . . . if I ever *had* to sell it . . ."

"Your point being?"

"Well, I mean, a new owner . . . surely . . ."

"Why wouldn't a new owner want the cross?"

"Well," I said, taking a hefty swig of my frosty see-through, "they might be, I don't know, Jewish, or . . . they might not *want* a big, a giant crucifix in their garden."

"Why not?"

I stared. He added, "It's a work of *art*."

"It is. It is absolutely that." [Clearing of throat.] "Still . . ."

"I wouldn't worry about it." I knew this formulation well. *I wouldn't worry about it* was WFB-speak for "The conversation is over." I was left with the impression I had committed lèse-majesté by suggesting that a future owner—Jewish, Muslim, Hindu, Amish, Zoroastrian—might be anything less than honored to have William F. Buckley's last remains in his garden, encased in an enormous bronze symbol of the crucified Christ. Certainly it would present the real estate broker with an interesting covenant clause. *Now, um, Mr. and Mrs. Birnbaum, you do understand that Mr. and Mrs. Buckley's ashes are to remain in the crucifix, in the garden. . . .*

No, I decided, driving up I-95, Sharon was the place for him. Sharon, where he'd grown up, where he'd been—by his own admission—happiest, between the ages of five and seven. For all his high sophistication and cosmopolitanism, there was in Pup an eternal inner boy. A teenage fan once wrote to him at *NR*, asking him what was his secret of happiness. He wrote back, "Don't grow up." It may have been this quality that propelled him to sail gleefully into northeast gales in his sailboat or leap into the cockpit of his Ercoupe barely knowing which knob was up or down. Yes, Sharon. It felt right. And he wasn't around to overrule me.

But, Christo, I want to be in the cross. We discussed it.

Sorry, old shoe, I'm taking you home, to Sharon. With the cross.

The last time I'd been with him there was the previous October. It was a fund-raiser for the local library, organized around the theme of "A Bevy of Buckleys," held on the grounds of Great Elm, once my grandfather and grandmother's house. Pup, Uncle Jimmy,* Aunt Pitts, Aunt Carol, and me, all gave readings from the aggregate Buckley oeuvre. We're a scribbly bunch: I count about ninety or so books among us—

------

*U.S. senator from New York, 1971–1977; justice, U.S. Court of Appeals for the District of Columbia, 1985–1996.

Pup, of course, having contributed the lion's portion.

The local newspaper had run a story promoting the event, and a line in it had caught my eye, affording me vast amusement: "The Buckleys are a well-known American family, William F. Buckley Jr. being arguably the most famous." I handed the clipping to Pup and counted silently as he read it, in anticipation of the reaction I knew would come. He looked up suddenly with a majestic, ironic frown (I would say a *semi*amused look) and said, " '*Ar-gu-ably*'?" We had a good laugh over that. My last memory of Pup at Great Elm was that Indian summer late afternoon, the sun slanting low over the green lawn, a large crowd hushed underneath the tent, as he read from a reminiscence about growing up there:

Outdoors it was very, very still, and from our bedroom we could hear the crickets and see the fire-flies. I opined to my sister Trish, age twelve, that when the wind dies and silence ensues, fireflies acquire a voice, and it is then that they chirp out their joys for the benefit of the nightly company, visible and invisible.

I turned into the driveway at Wallack's Point, the gravel crunching under the tires. The flag was at half-mast. Julian and Danny would have seen to that. I drove slowly past the garage study, where he'd died. His blue Greek yachtsman's hat was hanging on a hook, along with his cane and sweater. I remembered the phone call the previous April from Tina Brown after Mum died. She talked about when her mother died and she came across her reading glasses. "That really did it. I *completely* lost it." Now I thought, *Yeah, there's going to be a lot of losing it in the days ahead.*

Once they're both gone, your parents' house instantly turns into a museum. Every trace of them you see, you imagine inside a glass display case, along with a plaque or caption. *This red pen was used by William F. Buckley Jr. These sunglasses belonged to William F. Buckley Jr.* Danny had put Pup's wallet and watch on the desk in my room. *Wallet carried by William F. Buckley Jr. on the day he died. The watch is one of ten that he bought for companions aboard a sailboat he sailed in 1985 from Hawaii to New Guinea.* I picked up the wallet. I thought of all the times I'd seen him pull it from his back trousers pocket. He was a great reacher for the check at restaurants, Pup. He was always so generous that way.

That night, going to sleep, I looked out the window and the thought invariably came, *So, Pup, was it true, after all? Is there a heaven? Are you in it?* For all my doubts, I hoped he was. If he was, then at least I stood *some* chance of being admitted on a technicality, with the host of *Firing Line* up there arguing my case. I doubt St. Peter was any match for him. There were quite a number of editorial cartoons in the days ahead showing him arriving at the Pearly Gates. In one, St. Peter is whispering aside to an angel, "I'm going to need a bigger dictionary."

THERE WAS A LOT TO DO. I knew this already from Mum's death. *How many death certificates do we need? Fifty? Really?* It seemed odd we should need so many, given that his death was on the front page of every newspaper, on every TV news broadcast, and on a zillion Web sites. You'd have to be Osama bin Laden deep inside a rat hole in Tora Bora province not to know that *conservative icon* William F. Buckley Jr. had departed this vale of tears (a favorite phrase of his). Pup's family financial adviser had reported to me with amusement that an insurance company had sent the following letter: *Dear Mrs. Buckley, Thank you for sending your death certificate. The raised seal on it is not sufficiently raised. Please send us another death certificate with raised seal and we can then be able to begin processing your claim.* I'm surprised they didn't add a P.S.: *Have a nice day!* What can one say to such bureaucratic idiocy, other than "Whatever"? I'm thinking of having it engraved on my own headstone.

Danny and I drove to Leo P. Gallagher & Son Funeral Home. We both knew the way. Danny's dad had been taken there after he died. He had been wounded at Iwo Jima. Now my Greatest Generation father was there. The grown-ups were all leaving.

My old friend Chris the funeral director was punctilious and correct and soft-voiced. He allowed himself a mild smile when I greeted him with, "Wee'rre *back*."

I'd brought along a gray suit, white shirt, and a tie. The tie appeared conservative, but if you looked closely, you could see I LOVE MY WIFE repeated along the stripes and underneath, in backward-facing letters, BUT OH THAT BOAT! I'd puzzled over it, standing in his closet that morning. You don't want to send dear old dad off across the river Styx wearing a joke tie, and it's not a revocable decision, unless you're prepared, wearing a haunted expression on your face, to explain to the state of Connecticut exhumation officer that you need to dig him up because of "the tie." But in the end I thought, *Why not?* A conversation piece for Charon, a yachtsman himself. *Nice tie, Mr. Buckley.*

Mum had spent a considerable portion of her career as Mrs. William F. Buckley Jr. trying to make Pup look good—not just in the larger sense, but *presentable*. He was not a clothes-horse, my old man. Handsome, yes; slim-figured, to be sure; a bit of a slob? Um, yeah. Left to his own devices, he'd show up in khakis, Top-Siders, and a ratty blazer. Mum was forever saying, "*Bill*, you *cannot* go out dressed in that *ridiculous* attire," and then performing fashion triage on him, removing the tie with the stain, combing his hair, making him put on shoes that were shined, *for heaven's sake*. Her own sense of style was impeccable, and he delighted in it, even as he continued to shuffle along beside her, slightly unkempt.

The first time I was aware that Mum was, well, not like most other moms was when I was fourteen and under lock and key of the monks at boarding school. The day after parents' weekend, at which they had dutifully shown up, one of the older boys said to me, "Hey, Buckley, your mom's a piece of ass."

I stood there with face burning, trying to figure out what the appropriate response was. I wasn't actually sure if what he'd said constituted an insult, inasmuch as there was no higher accolade at Portsmouth Priory School, circa 1967, than "piece of ass." But it sounded like fightin' words, so I let fly. The scuffle was over in about five seconds, with me on my back on the floor and the older boy kneeling on my chest, explaining—sincerely, as I seem to remember—that he'd been referring to "her clothes." Well, okay, then.*

Further evidence that she was a bit different came from the school's switchboard operator—a fat, gossipy woman who regularly pored over the "Suzy Says" society column in the *New York Daily News*. "Your mutha

---

*I suppose these days she would be an MILF, but I am not going to go there.

went to a big party last night for Walter Cronkite!" she would yell out at me, into the crowded room where we checked our mailboxes. "She wore an Eves Saint Lawrent dress! Musta cost a *fortune*!" she bellowed, occasioning smirks from thirty other boys as I attempted invisibility.

It was around this time that the phrase *the chic and stunning Mrs. Buckley* entered our lives. It first appeared—we think—*not* in *Women's Wear Daily*, but in some other publication. Typically, Mum would use it when she was coming in from the garden—dirty, in jeans and black T-shirt, hair pulled back, no makeup. (She was never more beautiful to me than when she appeared thusly.) She'd say, "So much for the chic and stunning Mrs. Buckley."

Chic and stunning, she was, whether in Oscar de la Renta or her favorite Bill Blass. Pup was so proud of her, despite his own relative slovenliness. When she made the Best Dressed Hall of Fame, the Valhalla of Seventh Avenue, he called me up and said, "Be sure to make a big fuss. This is apparently a *very* big deal." I called her and made a big fuss. She changed the subject to the dog's bladder infection.

I asked her, many years later, where she had gotten her high sense of style, given that she had grown up in provincial British Columbia.[*] "From me," she said, not terribly interested in the subject. "I think I've always had an eye for my own sense of style. Mind you," she added heavily, "there have been *many* mistakes made. Fashion is fun,"

---

[*] Her father, Austin, a great bear of a man at six feet five and I don't know how many pounds, had always been a sharp dresser. "One time," she remembered, "the *Province* or the *Sun* ran a picture of Daddy on the front page and the caption underneath said, 'Sartorial Gem.' He was in such a rage that he went out to the farm and stayed there for three days."

she went on, "as long as you don't em-
barrass your husband. I remember last
year coming down the staircase at the
apartment in an outfit that I thought
was absolutely, startlingly gorgeous,
and your father said, 'Ducky, you look
absolutely gorgeous. Where's the rest
of the dress?' It was up to the kazoo."

I KNEW THE DRILL BY NOW. Chris slid
Jessica Mitford's price list across the
table. I wasn't going to haggle over
the embalming fee ($1,395). Or "dress-
ing and casketing of deceased" ($495).
Whatever. Burial is, of course, pricier
than cremation. There's a lot of item-
izing involved.

*Truck rental? Do we really need a
truck? He wasn't that big.*

*Actually, a "truck" is the rolling
stand that the casket rests on.*

*Aha. Well, yes, we'll definitely want
one of those.*

Finally, it was time to go into the next room and look at coffins. Death's showroom. All the latest models, a coffin for every taste. Some of them would not have been out of place in, say, a *Sopranos* episode.

I remembered years ago Pup telling me about going into Frank Campbell's in Manhattan to choose his father's coffin and the look of horror on the face of the salesman when he picked out the plainest. From his description of it, it sounded like something they'd put a John Doe in for burial in Potter's Field. I was six when Pup told me this story, and I vaguely remember asking him why he'd picked out such a plain one for his pup. Wasn't Grandfather rich? Yes, Pup said, but Grandfather was a humble man and the son of a very poor Texas sheriff, and he was *very* religious and didn't want God to think he needed to be buried in some $500 coffin. (This was 1958, bear in mind.)

There were some pretty plain coffins in Chris's showroom. I liked them, but Chris pointed out that they were for Jewish funerals. Jews—quite sensibly and admirably—shun funereal ostentation. (Either that, or they don't have any money left after the bar mitzvah.) I was tempted, but on closer inspection they looked almost as if they'd been hammered together by thirteen-year-olds during woodwork at summer camp. I imagined the Buckley family seeing Pup wheeled up the aisle of St. Bernard's in one of these jobs and murmuring about how that cheap SOB Christo was clearly trying to shave a few nickels off the tab. Danny and I settled on one made of pecan wood, a steal at $2,795.

"Now, I should let you know," Chris said, "pecan *is* a slightly heavier wood than some others." At first I didn't get it, but then I inferred that he was trying gently to point out that the coffin, fully loaded with Pup, who'd added a few pounds toward the end, might have the pallbearers popping hernias or collapsing as they groaned their way up the church steps. We did some quick math: six hundred pounds gross weight divided by eight (manly) pallbearers. No, that was doable. Sold.

We talked handles. This model, as others, came with or without handles. The coffin was grooved underneath on both sides so that pallbearers could grip it with their fingers and then heft it onto their shoulders, à la, say, Princess Diana. "It's an elegant approach," Chris said, "but I think in this case I would recommend handles. I could tell you stories." Yes, I said, let's go with handles. So we settled on that and went back to the conference room for the final tabulating. *Ka-chung, ka-chung, ka-chung.* . . . $11,105. But—remember, when it's your turn to do all this—tax-deductible! Perhaps someday, some congressman will bravely introduce a bill to remove the coffin deduction. I just hope I'm still alive to watch.

Finally, I said to Chris, "I'm going to want to put a few things in the coffin with him. Should I have you do that or is it something I can do when you bring him to the house for the wake?"

Chris nodded thoughtfully, frowned, shifted in his seat, and said in a very soft voice, "Before I answer, let me ask you: How frankly may I speak about the condition of Dad's remains?"

Dan and I glanced at each other. I said, "Shoot."

After the heart attack, he had lain on the floor for a while, facedown, before Julian found him. Blood had pooled. He looked "a little flushed." One doesn't want one's last glimpse of a parent to be a startling one that you can't ever get out of your head. My last glimpse of Mum, as she lay dying, is not the one I prefer to recall, but it comes to

319

me at times and I have to consciously put it back inside that locker in the hippocampus. I said, "If he's not looking his best, why don't I bring you the items and you can put them in."

He called me on my cell as Danny and I were driving home to say, "I was just with Dad, and good news, he's looking much better."

CHAPTER 19

Something I've Written for the Paper

I was about to leave for another meeting with Pup's lawyer. Our now-regular meetings consisted of a series of tutorials on the U.S. tax code, which seems to have developed over the years into a version of *The Da Vinci Code*. Figuring it out requires that you have a law degree and accounting degree;

alternatively, you can hire lots of people who do. Boiled down, it basically says, "We'll split it with you."

The phone rang. It was Sam Tanenhaus. Sam is Pup's biographer as well as editor of *The New York Times Book Review* and—since then—also the "Week in Review" section. I respected Sam. I'd been hugely impressed by his biography of Whittaker Chambers. Over a lunch, he'd told me he was now casting about for a new project. I'd said, *I've got one for you.* He'd leapt at the idea of writing a biography of WFB.

He said how sorry he was about the news. I thanked him. He said, "I'm calling because of something I've written for the newspaper."

"Yes?"

"A month ago I was out to Stamford and had dinner with your father. He told me that he was thinking about committing suicide."

"Uh-huh," I said.

"He said that he had discussed it with two priests and that they had told him that while it would be a sin, it would be a forgivable sin."

"Uh-huh. Well, he didn't commit suicide."

Pause. "Oh?"

"He died of a heart attack, Sam." I began to feel uncomfortable.

Pause. "So that's official?"

"Well, I have the death certificate here in front of me. It says under cause of death, 'Cardio-pulmonary arrest.' So, yes, that would appear to make it official."

"Well, that's why I called. I wanted to run it by you."

We rang off politely. My mind was reeling, but I went on with getting ready for the lawyer. Then, a few minutes later, I did a sort of mental double take. Had he said "something *I've written* for the paper"? I called him back.

"Sam," I said, "sorry, I'm a bit confused, with everything going on. Did you say you've already written something about this for the paper?"

"Yes."

"You mean, you're running a story about this?"

"Yes."

I took a breath. "Sam," I said, "if Pup told you that, and I don't doubt that he did, he was surely telling you that in your capacity as his biographer. Not as a reporter for *The New York Times*."

I saw a headline: IN FINAL DAYS, BUCKLEY CONTEMPLATED SUICIDE. Fine, but run that through the blogosphere and in thirty seconds it becomes BUCKLEY KILLED SELF. This is not mere filial hysteria on my part. This is America.

I wrote a book some years ago about the UFO world and learned a bit about what passes for "evidence" out there in this great, credulous nation of ours. I've read a little, too, about the Kennedy assassination. Roughly the same percentage of Americans believe in UFOs as believe that JFK was killed in a conspiracy. (Seventy-five.)

I knew Sam Tanenhaus to be a writer who gets his facts straight, but given the way America often connects its dots, I felt I had legitimate reason to fear that many would leap to the conclusion that the Lion of the Right had offed himself. And this was not a story I wanted to read and see rereported and twisted around as it zinged through cyberspace. And frankly, there was this, too: My father wasn't forty-eight hours dead. Why was Sam subjecting me to this?

After a pause, he said, "That's why I called you."

"Well, Sam," I said, shifting gears, "I think that were such a story to appear in the paper, a great number of people would be very upset."

"You do?"

"Yes. It's one thing if this appears on page 684 or whatever of your biography. You have every right to include it. But it's another matter if it appears in *The New York Times* as a news story. People are going to leap to conclusions, never mind what the death certificate says."

"I understand," he said. Pause. "But I should tell you that certain pressures are being brought to bear on me here, by Bill Keller and Jill Abramson." (Respectively, the top and number two editors at the *Times*.)

"Well then, Sam," I said, my voice now at about freezing point, "speaking as Pup's literary executor, I guess I can only say that you're just going to have to weigh those pressures along with others."

It was an explicit threat to shut the door on the William F. Buckley Jr. archive at Yale, consisting of 550 linear feet of his papers.* Sam had at this point invested half a dozen or so years on the project. Having his access cut off at this stage would be far from ideal, certainly not for the sake of one headline. Making threats isn't my thing, but I had no other weapon at hand.

"Okay," Sam said after a pause. "I will factor that in. And I appreciate your telling me all this."

And so we rang off. I was shaking. The world had been told, truthfully, that William F. Buckley had died at his desk while working. Now it was about to be informed by the newspaper of record that he had been in a suicidal state. I fast-forwarded to spending my life waving his death certificate at sniggerers and bloggers who would be saying, *Yeah? Well, that raised seal doesn't look so raised to me.* I had to stand up and pace around the room. I

---

*The Washington Monument is 555 feet high. That's a lot of linear feet.

was now—it appeared—at war with my father's biographer and, into the bargain, the editor of the nation's most influential book review.

A few hours later, as I was on my way in the car to Sharon to pick out a grave site, still sputtering with anger, Sam left a message on my voice mail. The tone was conciliatory and warm. He said, "I gave a lot of thought to what you said, and I've decided not to proceed with that story, and I wanted to tell you that and to thank you for talking to me about it." I e-mailed him back with reciprocal cordiality, thanking him.

A few months later, Sam's chapter on Pup's Yale years appeared as the cover story in *Yale Alumni* magazine. It was brilliant and fascinating, a perfect match of writer and subject. I can't wait to read the book.

CHAPTER 20

A Bit Much to Spring on a Lad with a Morning Head

❦

One morning, in the midst of negotiating with the padre in Sharon,
who, it turned out, had a strict policy
against "winter burials," the phone
rang. It was a well-known writer, an
old friend of my parents. He was so

upset that he could barely speak. He was literally spluttering over something that Pup's old adversary Gore Vidal had done.*

"I'm just appalled. I don't know what to say. I've known Gore since I was twenty. We all know he drinks and can be bitchy, but—this. It's disgusting. I don't know what could have gotten into him."

The item in question was from that morning's *New York Daily News*:

In an attack brutal even by Vidal standards, Gore writes on

———

*I'll leave it to Sam Tanenhaus to give the full details, but suffice it here to say that Vidal and WFB had clashed since the 1950s. Then, as commentators for ABC News during the 1968 Chicago Democratic convention, they *really* clashed, in an exchange that makes today's shout-fests on cable TV sound like kindergarten hissy-fits over spilt milk. Cleaning out my father's study after he died, I came across several long tons of files labeled "Vidal Legal." Well, it's a long story.

TruthDig.com that the National Review *founder was "a hysterical queen" and "a world-class American liar. . . . Buckley was often drunk and out of control." Vidal blames the "tired hacks" at* Newsweek *for letting Buckley's "creepy," "brain-dead" son, Christopher, talk them into a reverential cover story on his father. Vidal concludes, "RIP WFB—in hell."*

As Bertie Wooster would say, a bit much to spring on a lad with a morning head. I puzzled over this and could only conclude that the outpouring of admiration, respect, and affection for WFB had driven old Gore over the nearest cliff in a sputtering rage. This explosion of spittle and foam was somewhat at odds with the opening sentence of his most recent memoir: "As I move—I hope gracefully—

toward the door marked 'Exit . . .' " But there were more pressing matters to attend to: negotiating with the priest in Sharon. And there was the matter of the organist.

Pup was a serious amateur musician (piano, harpsichord) and devotee of Bach. He'd played harpsichord with the Phoenix Symphony Orchestra. Perhaps not his most successful hour onstage, but you had to hand it to him for chutzpah, and oh *Lord,* how he practiced. Three hours a day—for a *year.* He said to me, "I have never worked harder on anything, ever." For someone of his accomplishments, this was no whistling "Dixie."

He'd specified certain musical pieces for his funeral mass. The Sharon church organist was a sweet, elderly lady with a name like Prudence. When I called Prudence to go over the music, she didn't recognize any of the pieces. Not a one. I was reduced at one point to humming Bach's Air on a G String. There was a long silence at the other end. I hereby apologize to Prudence for putting her through such aural torture, but I was flailing. Doubtless she also would have preferred water-boarding to my rendition of Pachelbel's Canon in D Major, another tune unfamiliar to her. I had visions of Pup—friend of Rosalyn Tureck and Alicia de Larrocha, among other luminaries of the keyboard; who had once tricked the great Vladimir Horowitz into playing an impromptu recital—going into the empyrean to the sound of Prudence's "A Mighty Fortress Is Our God," sounding as if it were being played on kazoos. Desperate times call for desperate measures. I called Rick.

Rick Tripodi is an old friend of Pup's, an accomplished and sophisticated church organist possessed of a lovely, gentle, slightly mischievous touch. Rick has played for popes.

Rick, I said, *we have a problem*.

Rick got it right away. *No, no, no*, he said, *we can't let Dad go off that way!* He would intercede with Prudence and "Father."

He reported back a few hours later that Prudence had graciously, even eagerly, withdrawn. Rick would play and would bring along first-class vocalists for the "Ave Maria" and other pieces. "Father" couldn't have cared less; he didn't want anything to do with the music part.

The next day, Rick drove up to Sharon to inspect the facilities. He called.

That organ, he said. *My God! It must have been tuned last during the Truman administration. I've heard better-sounding hurdy-gurdies. But don't you worry about it. I'll think of something. Like maybe dynamite.*

Pup had served in the army in World War II, and though he hadn't stormed ashore at Omaha Beach, I liked the idea of giving him his military due.* "You need his DS-214," said Brian Kenney, the Sharon funeral director.

My advice to you is: If your dad—or mom—served in the military and you would like to have the honors at the funeral, find out *now* where that DS-214 (certificate of service) is. I spent *many* hours in the days ahead trying to find his. And I had a friend in the Pentagon, pretty high up, looking. And the *Pentagon* couldn't find it. (Well, that's not

---

*Pup was quite open about his lack of glorious military achievement. Under the category "What Did You Do in the War, Daddy?" he would tell, with vast amusement, of his greatest accomplishment: transporting one thousand Mexican-American recruits from San Antonio to San Luis Obispo. "My primary job was to keep them from getting venereal disease. And the only way to do it was, whenever the train stopped, to tell them that we would only be there for five minutes. That way they didn't have time to find the nearest bordello and get gonorrhea."

quite accurate: They located seventy-four William F. Buckleys who'd been discharged from the army in 1946; but none of them was *my* William F. Buckley.) Finally, after an archaeological dig so intensive it might have unearthed a second Troy, the elusive document was found—at the Stamford Town Hall, where he had deposited it in 1952.* So now we had that.

At which point Brian called to say that he'd just seen the weather report for Saturday: torrential, freezing rain. "I was just down to the cemetery," he said, pulling off several layers of rubber outerwear. "It's underwater."

There was a certain symmetry to it: just the sort of weather Pup liked to go sailing in! But at least it made moot my negotiations with "Father" over digging a winter grave. There wasn't much

---

*You leave it at Town Hall for tax purposes. Offspring of Greatest Generation, take note.

point in bringing in the "special" (translation: really expensive) equipment from Poughkeepsie if the grave was going to be a cisternby the time we tried to lower him in. But the church was booked, and Buckleys were flying in from everywhere. Brian volunteered in his springy, upbeat way, "I have just the place for him." An aboveground vault in another cemetery. "It's actually ideal," Brian said. I was unfamiliar with the logistics of body storage, but it seemed like an occasion to say, "Whatever."

The night before the funeral, I brought Pup home to Stamford for one last night in his home. He arrived by hearse, the pecan coffin covered with the American flag. We all choked up at that.

Once he had him situated in the dining room, Chris said, "Would you care to put in those items?" I nodded, and he opened the casket, and there was my Pup, in his gray suit with the white shirt and the I LOVE MY WIFE tie. He looked all right. But at the sight of him, we all lost it. I stroked his hair, careful not to touch his skin, which I knew, from contact with other bodies, can be a jolt, the hardness and the cold.

I'd transferred Mum's ashes from the brass plutonium canister to a red Chinese lacquered box I'd bought her years before for a birthday. I laid it on Pup's lap, so now they were together again. I put his rosary in his hands. Danny put in a jar of peanut butter. We looked at each other and simultaneously had the same thought. He went off and returned with the TV remote clicker and we put that in, too, and then we said one last good-bye, and I kissed him on the hair and we closed the lid and that was that. I pinned to the flag his Medal of Freedom. It looked heroic, and I was very proud of him.

Camilla, his English goddaughter, daughter of his great friend Sir Alistair

Horne, was on hand, and being British, she had taken charge of the flowers, rearranging and freshening them and adding gin to the water. *"Always add gin,"* she said. "They *adore* it." Camilla and Conor went off into the garden to smoke cigarettes. It was the first time I had seen my sixteen-year-old son with a cigarette, but there was something weirdly sweet about it, the two of them. I can't explain.

I put on a Whiffenpoofs CD and through the night played "Down by the Salley Gardens," a haunting melody set to the Yeats poem; and "Time After Time." A hundred people came and went. There *is* something to be said for having the body. You could, I suppose, hold a wake around an urnful of ashes, but it's not quite the same.

Everyone drank and ate and talked; much of it was merry. The rain sheeted against the windows. There were three priests, all friends of Pup's. At seven, when it was time, I said to Father Kevin, "Padre, care to do the mojo now?" He put on vestments. Two other priests joined him in saying prayers over the body. We all said an "Our Father." Father Kevin produced an aspergillum, the perforated bulb-shaped piece of metal that's dipped in the holy water to sprinkle a crowd or altar or coffin. I thought, watching as he wet the flag: *church and state, literally fused.*

I spent the night on the couch beside him, watching the candles guttering, listening to the rain and to the Whiffenpoofs, waking, stiff-necked, at four to find myself with a blanket over me. Camilla had come down in the night and covered me up.

Brian arrived next morning at eight and we loaded Pup into the hearse for his last drive up to Sharon. The hearse driver was Brian's father-in-law. We had a bit of a discussion over how to get to Sharon. Having made the drive perhaps three hundred times, I had my views; but he had his. He seemed quite certain, even adamant, so I said my mantra, "Whatever," and off we went, the hearse and eight cars following. Fifteen minutes into the drive, he turned onto a very unfamiliar road and then turned back toward Stamford. I cell-phoned, "Halt," to Brian, bringing our motorcade to a stop in a subdivision. Brian's father-in-law stoutly maintained that this was the way. "Whatever" has its limitations as a mantra.

At length, we got back on a correct road, at which point another aspect of Brian's father-in-law's driving became evident: his tendency to drive at eighty miles an hour in the rain while leading a procession of eight cars. This made for a lively caravan. We wove in and out of traffic on Route 22, blaring our horn occasionally at some innocent interloper. Lucy and Conor, beside me, held on for dear life. We made it in record time—a fitting homage, I suppose, to Pup's driving, which was never less than bracing.

Conor led his grandfather's coffin into the church. The pews were all filled with Buckleys. They had been well worn over the years by my family's knees. Lucy gave the first reading, Psalm 121, a favorite of her lovely Episcopalian family, who, charmingly, recite it aloud together every time a family member leaves on a trip. They call it the "Going Away" prayer.

I will lift up mine eyes to the hills, whence cometh my help. . . .

Conor did the second reading, from Ecclesiastes: "Vanity of vanity, saith the preacher, all is vanity."* Father Kevin gave the homily, in which he related a conversation he'd had with Pup some years earlier, on the subject of religious doubt. Father Kevin had said to Pup

___
*Private joke, but irresistible. I picked the readings.

at the lunch table, "Everyone at *some* point has doubts," and Pup had looked up from his borscht and said, "*I* never did."

I gave the eulogy and managed to lose it halfway through the first sentence. I recovered. When I told everyone about putting Mum in the coffin with him, saying, "It was the only way we'd get her back to Sharon," the church exploded with laughter. Mum had stopped coming up for Thanksgiving, well, a long time ago. At first she gave excuses, and then she stopped bothering even with those.

It was still pouring rain, so we did the military ceremony at the entrance to the church. A citation was read. The rifleman fired the volley. A bagpiper played "Amazing Grace." The flag was folded into a triangle and presented to me, with the thanks of a grateful nation. As it was handed to me, I heard sobs from behind me. The sergeant then presented Conor, standing beside me, with the empty cartridges from the rifle volley. "Cool," I whispered. Then a bugler sounded "Taps." Eight of us carried Pup out into the rain and loaded him back into the hearse. "Good-bye, my friend," said Danny, but it wasn't good-bye quite yet.

CHAPTER 21

There's a Mr. X, Apparently

Two mornings later, around nine, I was in bed, groggy, still on the first cup of coffee, Pup's dogs, Daisy and Rupert, chewing on each other at my feet—it seemed I had inherited them along with the other stuff—when the phone rang. A voice like a sonic boom:

"Is this Christopher Buckley?" I stammered yes, though I was sure my affirmation could only come as a letdown to someone with such an august voice. *"This is Car-di-nal Egan."*

I sat bolt upright. (Once an altar boy, always an altar boy.) "Yes," I said, trying frantically to remember the correct ecclesiastical title,"Your"— *Grace? Excellency? . . .quickly, man! —aha*—"Eminence."

Pup and I had discussed funeral arrangements some years ago. He'd said, "If I'm still famous, do it at Saint Patrick's.* If not, just do it in Stamford at Saint Mary's." To judge from the amount of ink and TV coverage his death was generating, he was very much "still famous." I'd sent word through a priest friend up the chain of command to the archdiocese, asking if the cathe-

---

*Cathedral, New York City.

dral might be available. Now the cardinal was calling. I was impressed by the fact that he'd dialed the number himself. None of that "I have His Eminence. Please hold, you miserable, sinful wretch." He was jovial and we joked about our common priest friend, whom he called (in jest) "a *thoroughly* disreputable character."

The pope was coming to town, and Easter loomed, but the cardinal found a spot on the cathedral calendar between this rock and that hard place. Mother Church can be a bureaucracy, to be sure, but when she moves, she moves with sureness.*

My first call was to Henry Kissinger. "Well, Henry," I said, "I seem to do little else these days but ask you to give

---

*Monsignor Eugene Clark, a former rector of Saint Patrick's, once quoted to me a line of Hillaire Belloc's about the Church:"What can one say of an institution ruled by eight hundred Italian clergymen?"

eulogies." He choked up and said that it would be an honor. I mean this as a compliment: For a Teuton with a steel-trap mind who was once more or less in charge of the world, Henry Kissinger has a heart of Jell-O. He is a certifiable member of the Bawl Brigade. He said he wasn't sure he'd be able to get through it. I said I'd sit in the front pew and make faces at him, if he'd do the same for me while I gave mine.

Word went out, and once again I was impressed with the celerity of our Internet age. Calls started coming in right away. I had decided to make the funeral open to the public, partly for good, partly for selfish reasons. I'd spent a great many man-hours on Mum's (of necessity) invitation-only memorial service, and it's no fun at all having to tell so-and-so that, no, sorry, Aunt Irma and Cousin Ida can't come, even if they were great admirers. I didn't want to play rope-line bouncer at St. Pat's. *You—okay. No, you can't come in. Oh, yes, Mr. Vidal, we've been expecting you. We have you right up front, next to Norman Podhoretz.*

The White House called. The president could not attend but would like Vice President Cheney to attend; moreover, he would like Vice President Cheney to speak. This was very thoughtful of the White House, but problematic. I envisioned two thousand people standing in line waiting to file through Secret Service metal detectors—and in the rain, almost certainly, since it had so far poured on every event connected with Pup's departure from this vale of tears. I said to the White House, *That's very thoughtful, and I am sincerely touched, but given the security requirements, perhaps it would be best to pass.* The White House called back and said, *We're not trying to "sell" you, but we do this all the time. The vice president attended Mike Deaver's and Jeane Kirkpatrick's services, and the disruption was minimal.*

I thought, *How I wish I could discuss this with Pup!* Pup just loved dilemmas of this kind. He would not have been blasé about being paid tribute to by a sitting vice president of the United States. But having myself been through many a Secret Service metal detector, I know very well that the disruption is not exactly "minimal," and the prospect of two thousand well-wishers having to empty their purses and being spread-eagled and wanded at the church door was not a consummation devoutly to be wished.

There was this, too: If Mr. Cheney came, he must be allowed to give remarks. But His Eminence had made it clear—gently—that there would be a limit of two eulogies. Over the years, there's been an inflationary tendency to pile on the eulogies, and Mother Church has started to put down her foot, on the perfectly reasonable principle that a funeral or memorial mass is a sacrament, not a meeting of the Friars Club. (*Let's save the roasting for the afterlife, shall we?*) The archbishop of Newark, New Jersey, had recently issued a ukase to the effect that there would be *no* eulogies at all in his archdiocese. (A bit harsh, methinks, but there it is.) At any rate, this left me with a Hobson's choice: Tell Henry Kissinger to step aside or give up my own slot. So there was nothing to do but decline the White House, as gently as I could.

There was a lively presidential campaign going on at the time (you may have heard about it). Pup being who he was, I wondered if we would be hearing from the presumptive Republican nominee, Senator John McCain. We never did, not a peep; odd, I thought, as he and I are old acquaintances. But presidential campaigns are, God knows, busy times.* Also odd, but very sweetly so, were the calls that did come in. One of the first was from Senator John Kerry. There was zero reason for him to have done that; it was a grace note, pure and simple. And then, one day as I was sitting in Pup's study feeling sorry for myself as I set about the (truly) enormous task of clearing it out, the phone rang. A gentle, sandpapery voice came on

------

*At a certain point, one begins—despite one's rational inclinations not to—to keep track of whom you hear from and whom you don't. My Irish friend Monie Begley says, "You never remember who came to the funeral, but you never forget who didn't." McCain's lack of any gesture at all did, I confess, smart a bit. It also left me to wonder about his organizational skills. At the most basic level, it was pretty poor staff work. But I may be oversensitive, having worked for George H. W. Bush, author of a hundred thousand handwritten notes, who routinely went out of his way to make the gracious gesture. When my mother died, I got a handwritten condolence letter from Al Gore, whom I'd met once, and only fleetingly, and who owed me absolutely nothing. Go figure.

the line: "I'm looking for Christopher Buckley." *Yes, this is he.* "Oh, Chris, it's George McGovern calling."

Pup and George McGovern were political antipodes, but they had become good friends a decade earlier after engaging in a series of public debates. I remembered Pup grinning one day over lunch, announcing, "Say, have I told you about my new best friend?" (Pause. Twinkle of the eyes.) *"George McGovern!* He turns out to be the single nicest human being I've ever met."

I recall my jaw dropping. When he ran for president in 1972, Pup had written and spoken some pretty tough things about George McGovern. As I winched my lower mandible back into place, I reflected that it wasn't all that improbable. Some of WFB's great friendships were with card-carrying members of the vast left-wing conspiracy: John Kenneth Galbraith, Murray Kempton, Daniel Patrick Moynihan, Ira Glasser (head of the ACLU, for heaven's sake), Allard K. Lowenstein, and so on. But there were piquant ironies to the friendship with McGovern.

As I've previously noted, Pup's boss at the CIA in 1951 was E. Howard Hunt. Howard was, as you know, arrested in June 1972 whilst jimmying open the door to the Democratic National Headquarters at the Watergate, in an effort, among other things, to put paid to George McGovern's presidential campaign. (A Pyrrhic bit of burglarizing, given what happened the following November, when only one state went for McGovern.) Pup had left the CIA's employ in 1952, but had remained friends with Hunt and was godfather to—and, indeed, trustee on behalf of—several of his four children.

As Watergate unfolded, I found myself, home on some weekends from college, in the basement sauna with Pup after dinner, listening as he confided his latest hush-hush phone call from

Howard. This was dramatic stuff. The calls would come at prearranged times, from phone booths. One night, Pup looked truly world-weary. Howard's wife, Dorothy, had just been killed in a commercial airline crash while on a mission delivering hush fund money.

It turns out that there's a safety deposit box . . .

I was twenty-one, an aspirant staff reporter on the *Yale Daily News*. Watergate was a huge story. No, make that the biggest story since the sack of Rome. *Oh*, how my little mouth salivated. Not that I could repeat a single word of any of this.

A safety deposit box?

There's a Mr. X, apparently. The way it works is this: I don't know his identity, but he knows mine. Howard has given him instructions: If he's killed—

Killed? Jesus. . . .

If something happens—whatever—

355

in that event, Mr. X will contact me. He has the key to the safety deposit box. He and I are to open it together.

And?

Pup looked at me heavily. *Decide what to do with the contents.*

Jesus, Pup.

Don't swear, Big Shot.

What . . . sort of contents are we talking about?

This next moment, I remember very vividly. Pup was staring at the floor of the sauna, hunched over. His shoulders heaved. He let out a sigh.

I don't know, exactly, but it could theoretically involve information that could lead to the impeachment of the president of the United States.

This conversation was taking place in December 1972. In the post-Clinton era, the word *impeachment* has lost much of its shock value, but back then, before the revelation of the Oval Office tapes or the defection of John Dean, the phrase *impeachment of the president of the United States* packed a very significant wallop. I was speechless. Pup was, to be sure, a journalist, but he took no pleasure in possessing this odious stick of dynamite. His countenance was pure Gethsemane: *Let this cup pass from me.* He would later recuse himself publicly, in the pages of his own magazine, from comment on Watergate, pleading conflict of interest based on his status as trustee of the Hunt children.

And now George McGovern, whose campaign had been the target of Howard Hunt and Gordon Liddy and the "plumbers," was on the phone from South Dakota, to condole someone he had never met and to say that he was planning to come to the memorial service, adding with what sounded like a grin, "If I can make my way through this fifteen-foot-high snowdrift outside my house." I put down the phone and wept.

CHAPTER 22

Home Is the Sailor

❀

I wrote my eulogy in Mum and Pup's bedroom early one morning as the sun was coming up over Long Island Sound. At that hour the mind is hard and focused, and I thought this would be the right atmosphere in which to write my words. I'll admit to performance anxiety: I would be following the Reverend George Rutler and Henry Kissinger, more or less the two most eloquent speakers on earth; and St. Patrick's Cathedral is Yankee Stadium. So as the sun rose, my thoughts were, *Let's try not to screw this up.*

Lucy and the kids and I spent the night before the service at the Yale Club, a few blocks from St. Pat's. We breakfasted in the dining room. At the next table was an old friend of Pup's who'd worked on his 1965 mayoral campaign.* He arched his eyebrows and reported that the "scuttlebutt" at a dinner the night before was that "Egan's pulled out."

I said I hadn't heard anything about that.

---

*Almost all the obituaries quoted his famous line: *Asked what he would do if he won, Buckley replied, "Demand a recount."*

"Apparently he went ballistic over having to share the altar with Monsignor Clark."

I hardly knew what to make of this. I did know that there were to be a number of priests at the altar concelebrating (as it is called) the mass and had indeed very much hoped that Monsignor Clark would be among them. Eugene Clark was a friend of Pup's from way, way back, a jolly, rubicund-faced Irish New Yorker with a keen intellect and mischievous wit. For years, he'd served as a sort of chaplain to the right wing. He'd been Cardinal Cooke's consigliere but had then somehow gotten on the wrong side of Cardinal O'Connor and been exiled to the Siberia of Westchester County for a few years. He'd made a comeback and been appointed rector of St. Patrick's, the equivalent, I suppose, of being sergeant at arms of the U.S. Congress. A big-deal job. He was at the altar in Washington in 1984 when

Lucy and I married. Everyone loved Monsignor Clark. And now you probably see where *this* is going. . . .

A few years ago, returning from an overseas trip, I called Lucy from the airport. She said, "Oh, gosh, isn't it awful about Monsignor Clark?" I braced. This was about the time of the endless (and repugnant) altar boy molestation scandals. I groaned, "Oh, not Monsignor Clark!" Lucy quickly added, "No, no—it was his secretary. A woman." I practically burst out laughing. "Oh, well, for heaven's sake, what's all the fuss, then?" But it was a big fuss: a front-page tabloid-level fuss and the end of Monsignor Clark's career as rector of St. Patrick's.

Pup, who had always been legendarily loyal to his friends, had—oddly—written an entire column about it, rehashing the whole sorry mess and in the process wagging a finger at his old friend. I had sent word that I would be pleased, even delighted, to see Monsignor Clark among the other priests at the altar. But now, as I set off for St. Patrick's, I was left to wonder if I had created some fracas in the cathedral that had sent His Eminence stomping off in a crimson huff—a real confidence builder as you set off to the church to eulogize Dad.

It was—surprise—raining as we walked to the cathedral. As we turned the corner of Madison and headed west down 49th Street, I thought back to another day, in October 1965, when I walked down this same sidewalk, hand in hand with my father.

The occasion was the visit of Pope Paul VI, a papal mass. But there was something else going on, I soon realized, as the police steered Pup and me down the cordoned-off sidewalk and we began walking, almost alone, down the long sidewalk toward the cathedral's entrance. The mayoral campaign was in full swing. Pup waved to the large crowds on the other side of the cordon. The crowd responded, and it was abundantly clear that they were by no means unanimous in their support of the candidate for the Conservative Party. Boos, jeers, catcalls. It got pretty raucous. Pup clutched my hand tightly. The shouts got louder and louder, coarser and coarser. I was thirteen. It seemed a very long way from Madison Avenue to Fifth Avenue. Pup gripped my hand tighter and grinned back, as candidates must while being pelted with verbal rotten vegetables. As we reached the end of the block, I heard a voice shouting: "Buckley, you asshole! I hate your fucking guts!" I'd been keeping my eyes on the ground, but this voice sounded . . . familiar. I turned, and our eyes met: It was a seventh-grade classmate of mine from St. David's. I don't think he'd seen me as he spat out his epithets. Now he did, and he went ashen-faced; but no more than I. The rest of the event passed more pleasantly, and I got my first up-close look at a pope, in a pew sitting next to actor-turned-senator George Murphy.

LUCY AND THE KIDS AND I made our way to our seats. It was a full house, twenty-two hundred. There was George McGovern, having braved the snowdrifts: frail, cancer-ridden, smiling. Former mayor Ed Koch—*Hiya, howyadoing?*—jimmied his way into our family pew. Senator Joe Lieberman was there. Congressman Chris Shays was the only Republican I saw there. Just before the service began, in came Kitty Galbraith, John Kenneth Galbraith's ninety-five-year-old widow, supported by all three of her sons and various granddaughters; a more valiant sight, I've never seen. Christopher Hitchens, having dashed off a plane from Grand Rapids, trailing his roller bag, slipped into the last empty seat. Christopher, bosom friend of thirty years, our most eloquent atheist, was observed belting out John Bunyan's "He Who Would Valiant Be."

I've dumped all over Mother Church for her tepid liturgies and "kumbaya" and the rest, but she can rise to an occasion, and she sure did on this day. Rick Tripodi and Donald Dumler were at the organ, accompanying the St. Patrick's Cathedral Choir. They gave us Bach's Air on a G String and Adagio in A Minor; the "Kyrie" and "Sanctus" and "Agnus Dei" from Tomás Luis de Victoria's *Missa*; St. Bernard of Cluny's "Jerusalem the Golden"; "Nearer, My God, to Thee." During communion, Palestrina's "Ego Sum Panis Vivus" was followed by a gorgeous, triumphant Albinoni Adagio in G Minor, whose deep bass notes sounded as though they were issuing from the *Titanic*'s smokestacks. The pews were practically vibrating. Then came Holst's "I Vow to Thee, My Country"; and finally, for the postlude, the one piece that I had asked for: the joyful, high pipe notes of the third movement of the Brandenburg Concerto No. 2, familiar to many Americans as the theme music to *Firing Line*.

Father Rutler officiated. His Eminence, as it turned out, had not—for heaven's sake—huffed off on account of having to share the altar with a naughty monsignor. He'd been called to Rome—*called to Rome*, that pungent phrase—in connection with the imminent papal visit. Monsignor Clark was not at the altar, anyway; but he was there somewhere, for I was able to give him a hug at the reception afterward. I counted twenty priests around the altar. There ought to be a collective noun for that—a "bless" of priests? It was—to use the word literally—spectacular.

Henry Kissinger, his voice cracking at various points, eulogized his old friend.

"He wrote," he said, "as Mozart composed, by inspiration; he never needed a second draft. A man of such stunning versatility might have proved daunting to those around him. Yet we mourn him for his civility even to adversaries, his conviviality, his commitment, and, above all, the way he infused our lives with a very special presence. . . .

" 'I am a Burkeian,' he would say. 'I believe neither in permanent victories nor in permanent defeats.' But he did believe deeply in permanent values. 'We must do what we can,' he wrote to me, 'to bring hammer blows against the bell jar that protects the dreamers from reality. The ideal scenario is that pounding from without we can effect resonances, which will one day crack through to the latent impulses of those who dream within, bringing to life a circuit that will spare the republic.' "

He touched on Pup's faith: "Over a decade ago, Bill and I discussed the relationship of knowledge to faith. I surmised it required a special act of divine grace to make the leap from the intellectual to the spiritual. In a note, Bill demurred. No special epiphany was involved, he argued. There could be a spiritual and intellectual drift until, one day, the eyes opened and happiness followed ever after. Bill noted that he had seen that culmination in friends. He did not claim it for himself. . . .

"Those of us who have grown old with Bill know better. We will forever remember how we were sustained by Bill's special serenity, the culmination of a long and very private quest. The younger generation, especially of his collaborators whom he so cherished, was inspired by the inward peace Bill radiated, which he was too humble and, in a deep sense, too devout to assert except by example. In the solitude of parting, all of us give thanks to a benign Providence that enabled us to walk part of our way with this noble, gentle, and valiant man who was truly touched by the grace of God."

I took the podium and said, "Pope Benedict will be saying mass here in two weeks. I was told that the music at this mass for my father would in effect be the dress rehearsal for the pope's. I think that would have pleased him, though doubtless he'd have preferred it to be the other way around. . . .

"On the day he retired from *Firing Line* after a thirty-three-year-long run, *Nightline* did a show to mark the occasion. At the end, Ted Koppel said, 'Bill, we have one minute left. Would you care to sum up your thirty-three years in television?' To which my father replied, 'No.' Taking that cue, I won't attempt to sum him up in my few minutes up here. . . .

"José Martí famously said that a man

must do three things in life: write a book, plant a tree, have a son. I don't know that my father ever planted a tree. Surely whole forests—enough to make Al Gore weep—were put to the ax on his account. But he did plant a great many seeds, and many of them, grown to fruition, are here today. Quite a harvest, that.

"It's not easy coming up with an epitaph for such a man. I was tempted by something Mark Twain once said: 'Homer's dead, Shakespeare's dead, and I myself am not feeling at all well.'

"Years ago, he gave an interview to *Playboy* magazine. Asked why he did this, he couldn't resist saying, 'In order to communicate with my sixteen-year-old son.' At the end of the interview, he was asked what he would like for an epitaph and he replied, 'I know that my Redeemer liveth.' Only Pup could manage to work the Book of Job into a Hugh Hefner publication.

"I finally settled on one, and I'll say the words over his grave at sunset, in Sharon, when we lay him to rest. They're from a poem he knew well, each line of which, indeed, seemed to have been written just for him:

Under the wide and starry sky
Dig the grave and let me lie:
Glad did I live and gladly die;
And I laid me down with a will.

This be the verse you 'grave for me:
'Here he lies where he long'd to be;
Home is the sailor, home from sea,
And the hunter home from the hill.'"

CHAPTER 23

Postlude

I began this book on the note of becoming an orphan, so perhaps it makes sense to return to that theme in this penultimate chapter. I type this now a year and a half after Mum died and over half a year since Pup left. Some dust has settled, some continues to swirl.

Postlude

I think about them every day, and not—I venture—because I have been at work on this book. Writing it (I suspect) was intended to enable catharsis; now, as I reach the end, it seems to me that I may have written it out of a more basic need: as an excuse to spend more time with them before letting them go—if, indeed, one ever really lets them go. So instead of a working-it-out exercise, perhaps this is just a black-and-white album of memories, in which the unfond memories can be leeched of bitterness and settle quietly and stingless like scattered autumn leaves on the soft forest floor. It feels to me like that, at any rate.

Orphanhood proceeds, meanwhile, tanned (as Leon hoped) and otherwise. People are wonderfully solicitous. *How are you doing?* they say, putting a sympathetic emphasis on the last word, to show that they actually mean it. Suddenly—writing this—I remember Pup telling me years and years ago about a book by Wilfred Sheed with the title *People Will Always Be Kind*. I've never read it; it's just that somehow everything one way or the other seems to remind me of Pup or Mum.

It comes in waves, my fellow orphans will probably inform you. One moment you're doing fine, living your life, even perhaps feeling some primal sense of liberation—*I can stay out as late as I want and I don't have to make my bed!*—and then in the next, boom, there it is. It has many ways of presenting (as doctors say of a disease). Sometimes it comes in the form of a black hole inside you, sucking the rest of you into it; other times it's a sense of disconnection, as if you had been holding your mother's hand in a crowd and suddenly she let go, and now here you are, not alone, exactly, but it *feels* alone. Yesterday on television, I watched young children pay tribute to their fathers and mothers who died in the two towers on 9/11 when the children were four, five, or six years old. I can't imagine *their* sense of orphaning. Prattling on about mine, at age fifty-five, seems pathetic by contrast. As Mum would say, "Oh, do pull yourself together and stop carrying on in this fashion." Yes, Mum. I'm almost done.

Advice? Let's see. Having been through the experience, one really ought to return with a pointer or two. There are seventy-seven million of us boomers; many of us have already lost the 'rents, and the rest of us will be going through the experience later if not sooner.

The only *concrete* bit of advice—don't laugh—is: Have Mom and Dad prenegotiate the funeral expenses. I've told my story of the funeral home price list to a number of people, and one of them said, nodding, "Mom negotiated *her* cremation ahead of time. You'd be surprised how much the price comes down." This sounds like very good advice, so I pass it along. And if that doesn't work, when Mom or Dad begins to fail, get them to Belfast, Maine. (See footnote, page 70.)

As to the "you're next" aspect that I mentioned in the preface: There's not a whole lot to be done on this score, other than the usual boring things—don't smoke, don't eat anything that tastes really good, and spend most of the rest of your life on a StairMaster. In a few days, I'll come up on the twentieth anniversary of the day I gave up smoking, and that's a good feeling. I rather like breathing. Still, I wonder if our obsession with longevity is entirely . . . healthy.

"Perhaps the best cure for the fear of death," wrote William Hazlitt, "is to reflect that life has a beginning as well as an end. There was a time when we were not; this gives us no concern—

why then should it trouble us that a time will come when we shall cease to be?"

Well, any English major can quote all sorts of people and talk a good game. Ask me how I feel when Dr. Hughes tells me, "I'd like to do another PSA test, if you don't mind."

My dear friend Rust Hills, who died this summer (in Belfast, Maine), was a great fan of Michel de Montaigne. Montaigne spent a *lot* of time thinking about death. (This seems to be a French trait.) Rust died a darn good death at age eighty-three: One August day, in the company of his wife and daughter and grandson, in a house by the sea, he had a Scotch, a bowl of clam chowder, and a slice of blueberry pie and—died. Not a bad way to go. Put me down for the same.

I couldn't find anything in Montaigne about Scotch, clam chowder, or blueberry pie, but I found this: "The ceaseless labor of your life is to build the house of death." Probably too downbeat-sounding by American smiley-face standards to end up on a refrigerator magnet, but *pas mal*. I guess one way or the other, it boils down to being able to look the Reaper right in the eye with a smile and say, "Oh, puhleeze." I bet that was how Mum did it, adding, "And what, pray, is that *absurd* costume supposed to indicate?"

Yesterday, I was driving behind a belchy city bus on the way back from the grocery store and suddenly found myself thinking (not for the first time) about whether Pup is in heaven. He spent so much of his life on his knees in church, so much of his life doing the right thing by so many people, a million acts of generosity. I'm—I shouldn't use the word—dying of curiosity: How did it turn out, Pup? Were you right after all? Is there a heaven? Is Mum there with you? (Grumbling, almost certainly, about the "inedible food.") And if there is a heaven and you are in it, are you thinking, *Poor Christo—he's not going to make it.* And is Mum saying, *Bill, you have got to speak to that absurd creature at the Gates and* tell *him he's got to admit Christopher. It's too ridiculous for words.*

Even in my dreams, they're looking after me. So perhaps one is never really an orphan after all.

CHAPTER 24

The Hunter Home
from the Hill

Three days after the memorial
service at St. Patrick's, and a week
shy of the first anniversary of Mum's
death, Danny and I loaded the heavy
bronze cross into the back of the van
and drove up to Sharon. For the first
time since February 27—it seemed—it

wasn't raining. The sun was shining. It was a beautiful Connecticut spring day.

Aunt Pitts and Uncle Jimmy and the funeral director and two grave diggers were waiting for us along with the hearse, at the little cemetery by the brook. Brian the funeral director had called me on my cell as Danny and I were on the road, to report with professional alarm in his voice that the cover on Pup's pecan coffin had "split" somewhat during his stay above-ground. It didn't sound like a Faulknerian-level coffin disaster, so I said not to worry. Pup wouldn't have. As to burying him *in corpore* in Sharon, I think he'd have forgiven my final disobedience. Doubtless Mum will haunt me to the end of my days for bringing her back to Sharon, but she'll make a great ghost and I can't wait to be haunted by her.

With the help of Brian's teenage son and the grave diggers, Danny and

I lifted Pup and Mum from the hearse and carried them across the graves of his sisters Mary Ann (buried here in 1928, having lived for one day), Maureen (1964), Aloise (1967), and Jane (2007). I could hear Jane saying with an unmistakable hint of triumph, *Why, Pat, what a pleasant surprise.* And Mum replying heavily, *Yes,* isn't *it?*

Pup's English goddaughter, Camilla, who had poured gin into all the flowerpots at the wake, sent a beautiful spray of white flowers all the way from Wales, with a note inscribed in her own hand: *Good night, sweet prince, and flights of angels sing thee to thy rest.* So between my e-mail on the morning he died and Camilla's note, Pup went off well bracketed with quotes from *Hamlet.* One could do worse.

We set the coffin on the straps and lowered them into the spring-warm earth. Birds sang in the budding branches. The late afternoon sun slanted through the still-bare limbs. We each took a handful of earth and sprinkled it into the grave, said our various silent farewells, and left them there, together, in each other's arms.

There's a Greek myth that Pup loved to retell, of Philemon and Baucis. They were a devoted old couple who provided hospitality to Jupiter and Mercury, traveling incognito. The gods then revealed themselves in all their glory, smote the crap out of everyone who *hadn't* shown them hospitality, and rewarded the old couple by turning their hut into a gorgeous temple. They asked them if there was anything else they wanted. Philemon and Baucis replied that, yes, they'd like to be together for all eternity. So the gods changed them into two trees whose limbs intertwined. It's a lovely story.

William F. Buckley Jr. and Patricia Taylor Buckley were, I think it's safe to say, a more complicated package than old Philemon and Baucis—and almost certainly more fun to have dinner with. But their devotion to each other, however complex, was no less intense, no less enduring, and no less deserving of celebration. I hope this book, for all its complexities, is a testament to that devotion. They were . . . well, I'm out of words, finally. They were my Mum and Pup.

—September 12, 2008
Washington, D.C.

ACKNOWLEDGMENTS

Thank you, once again, my very dear Mr. Karp. Thanks, yet again, dear Binky. Thank you, beloved Lucy. Bless you, Pitts. You, too, Jolie. Thank you, John Tierney, Greg Zorthian, Frances Bronson, Jack Fowler, Linda Bridges, Dusty Rhodes. At Twelve (this is starting to sound like an interminable Oscar speech): the indefatigable Obi-Wan, Cary Goldstein, and the indispensable and unflagging Harvey-Jane Kowal, and Sona Vogel. And, of course, once again, the Faithful Hound Jake, who kept the perimeter secure.

TWELVE

MISSION STATEMENT

TWELVE was established in August 2005 with the objective of publishing no more than one book per month. We strive to publish the singular book, by authors who have a unique perspective and compelling authority. Works that explain our culture; that illuminate, inspire, provoke, and entertain. We seek to establish communities of conversation surrounding our books. Talented authors deserve attention not only from publishers, but from readers as well. To sell the book is only the beginning of our mission. To build avid audiences of readers who are enriched by these works—that is our ultimate purpose.

For more information about forthcoming
TWELVE books, you can visit us at
www.twelvebooks.com